Beyond Borders

The Global Impact of Rhino Horn Trafficking

Eshan Sheroy

Spectra Enterprise

CONTENTS

Introduction

1. Overview of the rhino horn trafficking crisis
2. The global significance of the issue
3. Purpose of the book: Unveiling the interconnectedness and far-reaching consequences

Chapter 1 The Rhino and Its Horn
1.1 Rhino species and distribution
1.2 Significance of rhino horns in traditional medicine and cultural practices
1.3 The misconception surrounding the medicinal properties of rhino horns

Chapter 2 Rise of Rhino Horn Trafficking
2.1 Historical context of rhino horn trade
2.2 Factors fueling the demand for rhino horns
2.3 Criminal networks and their involvement

Chapter 3 Impact on Rhino Populations
3.1 Statistics on rhino population decline
3.2 Ecological consequences of rhino poaching
3.3 Efforts and challenges in rhino conservation

Chapter 4 Human Cost of Trafficking
4.1 Involvement of local communities in poaching
4.2 The impact on the lives of rangers and conservationists
4.3 Rise of organized crime and violence associated with rhino horn trade

Chapter 5 Socioeconomic Ramifications
5.1 Economic impact on countries with rhino populations
5.2 The role of corruption in exacerbating the issue

INTRODUCTION

In the shadows of the African savannas and Asian prairies, a quiet battle is unfurling — one that rises above geographic limits, social partitions, and environmental domains. Past Boundaries: The Worldwide Effect of Rhino Horn Dealing dives into the complex snare of rhino horn dealing, an emergency that resounds across mainlands, influencing biological systems, networks, and the actual quintessence of biodiversity. This far reaching investigation tries to disentangle the multi-layered elements of an emergency that stretches out past the quick domains of protection, extending its limbs into the unpredictable texture of global relations, social practices, and financial designs.

Authentic Introduction: The Charm of Rhino Horns

The charm of rhino horns follows back hundreds of years, entwining with assorted societies and conviction frameworks. Looking at the verifiable setting gives an establishment to understanding how these lofty animals developed from worshipped images to imperiled casualties of unlawful exchange. From old restorative practices to contemporary superficial points of interest, the excursion of rhino horns winds around a story that traverses ages and mainlands.

The Rhino Species and Their Dubious Presence

A nitty gritty investigation of the different rhino species — Dark, White, Indian, Sumatran, and Javan — makes way for understanding the remarkable difficulties each countenances. The geological dispersion of these species and their natural importance lay the basis for appreciating the more extensive ramifications of their decay because of poaching.

Meaning of Rhino Horns in Customary Medication and Social Practices

Integral to the worldwide effect of rhino horn dealing is its well established association with customary medication and social practices. This part digs into the convictions and customs that support the interest for rhino horns, investigating the social scenes where these practices continue and evaluating their commitment to the heightening emergency.

The Misguided judgment Encompassing the Restorative Properties of Rhino Horns

Expanding on the social setting, this part investigates the logical veracity of the indicated restorative properties credited to rhino horns. By destroying legends and introducing exact proof, the point is to enlighten the unmistakable difference between customary convictions and the biological reality, testing the very establishments supporting the interest.

Ascent of Rhino Horn Dealing: Authentic Setting

A verifiable examination unwinds the foundations of the cutting edge rhino horn exchange, following its development from restricted practices to a worldwide criminal undertaking. Understanding the verifiable setting gives experiences into the interconnected variables that have energized the ascent of a rewarding, illegal market.

Factors Energizing the Interest for Rhino Horns

Inspecting the interest side of rhino horn dealing clarifies the variables that support this complicated organization. Monetary drivers, social insights, and international impacts merge to make an unpredictable embroidery of interest that rises above borders, representing an impressive test for traditionalists and policymakers the same.

Criminal Organizations and Their Association

At the core of rhino horn dealing lies a snare of coordinated wrongdoing that traverses the globe. This part dives into the designs and tasks of criminal organizations, investigating how they exploit administrative holes, influence innovation, and adjust to authorization endeavors. Disentangling these organizations is fundamental to upsetting the illegal exchange.

Influence on Rhino Populaces: A Protection Emergency

The protection account unfurls in this part, specifying the staggering effect of poaching on rhino populaces. From plunging numbers to hereditary difficulties, the repercussions of unrestrained dealing stretch out a long ways past individual creatures, undermining the actual presence of whole species.

Measurements on Rhino Populace Decline: A Quantitative Viewpoint

Evaluating the size of the emergency, this segment gathers and breaks down measurements on rhino populace decline. By looking at local patterns, species-explicit information, and the ramifications for biodiversity, an extensive outline arises, giving a quantitative focal point through which to measure the seriousness of the preservation emergency.

Biological Results of Rhino Poaching

Past the prompt danger to rhino populaces, the biological outcomes of poaching echo through environments. Disturbances to biological equilibrium, flowing impacts on different species, and the change of scenes are analyzed in this part, revealing insight into the more extensive environmental repercussions of rhino horn dealing.

Endeavors and Difficulties in Rhino Protection: A Worldwide Viewpoint

This segment gives a far reaching outline of worldwide endeavors to monitor rhinos. It investigates preservation methodologies, mechanical advancements, and local area based drives while examining the industrious difficulties looked by progressives, going from asset imperatives to political intricacies.

Human Expense of Dealing: Effect on Officers and Preservationists

The human cost of fighting rhino horn dealing is investigated here, zeroing in on the encounters of officers and traditionalists who explore the bleeding edges. From actual dangers to mental weights, understanding the penances made by those devoted to safeguarding rhinos adds a strong aspect to the story.

Association of Neighborhood People group in Poaching: Complex Elements

This segment investigates the perplexing elements between neighborhood networks and poaching exercises. Adjusting the requirement for preservation with the financial real factors of networks living in nearness to rhino environments, it investigates how cooperative methodologies can adjust protection objectives to local area prosperity.

The Effect on the Existences of Officers and Progressives: A Profound Excursion

Diving into the profound and mental cost claimed on those took part in the fight against rhino horn dealing, this segment refines the account. Individual stories, challenges confronted, and the strength of those on the cutting edge highlight the gravity of their responsibility and the human component of protection.

Ascent of Coordinated Wrongdoing and Brutality Related with Rhino Horn Exchange

Looking at the nexus between rhino horn dealing and coordinated wrongdoing, this segment investigates the heightening of brutality inside the exchange. From poaching occurrences to the more extensive crook organizations, the interweaving of criminal operations makes an unpredictable scene that requests multi-layered intercession.

Financial Implications: Disentangling the Strings

The financial effect of rhino horn dealing stretches out past preservation to influence networks, economies, and public dependability. This segment analyzes the financial repercussions, investigating how unlawful exchange disturbs jobs, encourages defilement, and sustains patterns of neediness in impacted areas.

Financial Effect on Nations with Rhino Populaces: Difficult exercise

Dissecting the monetary components of rhino horn dealing at a public level, this part thinks about the more extensive effect on nations with rhino populaces.

The sensitive harmony between momentary monetary increases and the drawn out manageability of regular assets is investigated, encouraging policymakers to think about preservation as indispensable to financial flourishing.

The Job of Debasement in Compounding the Issue: A Fundamental Examination

Debasement is an unavoidable issue in the battle against rhino horn dealing. This part digs into the fundamental foundations of defilement, analyzing how it invades policing, designs, and global establishments. Addressing defilement becomes central to disturbing the organizations that support unlawful exchange.

Worldwide Financial Ramifications of Unlawful Natural life Exchange: A Full scale Point of view

Zooming out to a macroeconomic point of view, this segment investigates how unlawful untamed life exchange, including rhino horn dealing, resounds through the worldwide economy. The interconnectedness of business sectors, the job of customers, and the more extensive monetary ramifications make a convincing case for worldwide joint effort in handling this worldwide test.

Worldwide Reaction: A Source of inspiration

Surveying the global reaction to rhino horn dealing, this part inspects existing legitimate systems, peaceful accords, and cooperative drives. It examines the viability of these reactions, distinguishes holes, and requires a bound together worldwide front against untamed life wrongdoing.

Existing Lawful Systems and Peaceful accords: An inside and out Investigation

Exploring the complexities of existing lawful systems and peaceful accords, this part fundamentally evaluates their viability in tending to rhino horn dealing. From Refers to provincial arrangements, the investigation expects to perceive the qualities and shortcomings that shape the legitimate scene.

Victories and Disappointments in Fighting Rhino Horn Dealing: Examples Learned

Expanding on the examination of worldwide reactions, this segment assesses the triumphs and disappointments in battling rhino horn dealing. Examples gained from past endeavors give significant experiences to molding future procedures and intercessions.

The Requirement for Cooperative Endeavors Among Countries: A Discretionary Objective

Underlining the political goal, this part advocates for upgraded cooperative endeavors among countries. Conciliatory procedures, data sharing, and joint tasks are investigated as fundamental parts of a worldwide reaction to rhino horn dealing.

Imaginative Methodologies: Kicking off something new

This part investigates inventive ways to deal with battling rhino horn dealing, from the utilization of innovation to local area based preservation drives. By featuring effective developments and arising patterns, it energizes a dynamic and versatile reaction to the advancing difficulties presented by natural life wrongdoing.

Innovation and Its Part in Protection and Hostile to Poaching Endeavors: A Mechanical Boondocks

Analyzing the state of the art job of innovation in protection, this segment investigates how headways in simulated intelligence, blockchain, and checking advances are reshaping against poaching endeavors. The combination of innovation offers additional opportunities for following, safeguarding, and figuring out rhino populaces.

Local area Based Preservation Drives: A Grassroots Upheaval

Local area based preservation drives become the dominant focal point in this part, stressing the force of nearby networks in shielding rhinos. By investigating effective models and grassroots developments, the account highlights the significance of comprehensive and feasible protection rehearses.

Imaginative Methodologies to Diminish Interest for Rhino Horns: Molding Purchaser Conduct

Moving the concentration to request decrease, this segment investigates imaginative techniques to reshape purchaser conduct. From superstar supports to inventive advertising efforts, it looks at how social discernments can be changed to deter the utilization of rhino horns.

Stories from the Bleeding edge: Accounts of Boldness and Penance

Fixating on private accounts, this part exposes the narratives of people on the bleeding edge of rhino preservation. Through their eyes, the account catches the boldness, penances, and unfaltering commitment that characterize the human experience inside the fight against rhino horn dealing.

Individual Stories of People Influenced by Rhino Horn Dealing: A Human Point of view

Moving the concentration to those straightforwardly affected, this segment investigates the accounts of people whose lives have been interwoven with the repercussions of rhino horn dealing. By adapting the account, it tries to cultivate compassion and develop comprehension of the human expense related with natural life wrongdoing.

Accounts from Policing, and Nearby People group: A Mosaic of Viewpoints

Uniting assorted viewpoints, this part accumulates accounts from policing, preservationists, and neighborhood networks. By winding around together these differed stories, the part means to give a mosaic of experiences into the intricacies and difficulties looked in the battle against rhino horn dealing.

Motivational Accounts of Effective Protection and Hostile to Dealing Drives: Encouraging signs

In the midst of the difficulties, this part celebrates motivational accounts of effective protection and against dealing drives. By featuring situations where purposeful endeavors have yielded positive results, the story means to motivate and ingrain a feeling of expectation for what's to come.

Looking Forward: Future Possibilities for Rhino Populaces

As Past Lines closes, it turns its look to the future, surveying the possibilities for rhino populaces. In this last segment, the story looks at progressing preservation endeavors, arising patterns, and the aggregate vision expected to get a maintainable future for these glorious animals.

Through this far reaching investigation, Past Lines looks to enlighten the perplexing woven artwork of rhino horn dealing. By navigating geological, social, and natural limits, this story tries to move an aggregate obligation to the protection of rhino populaces and the environments they possess. In the sections that follow, the excursion unfurls, welcoming perusers to dive into the core of an emergency that stretches out past lines, repeating a source of inspiration for the conservation of our planet's regular legacy.

1. Overview of the rhino horn trafficking crisis

The emergency of rhino horn dealing remains as a piercing demonstration of the perplexing exchange of natural, social, and monetary elements that undermine the actual presence of these brilliant animals. Rhinos, notable images of the wild, are blockaded by a determined flood of poaching, driven by the voracious interest for their horns. This outline reveals insight into the multi-layered components of the emergency, from its verifiable roots to its contemporary worldwide effect, investigating the perplexing web that envelops rhino preservation and the unlawful exchange their horns.

1. **Verifiable Introduction: The Appeal of Rhino Horns**
   The foundations of rhino horn dealing are profoundly implanted ever, where these lofty animals once meandered openly across assorted scenes. Rhino horns, once venerated as images of solidarity, status, and restorative properties, became desired wares. Authentic records follow their utilization in customary medication, especially in specific Asian societies, where they were accepted to have recuperating properties. After some time, these social insights developed, adding to the contemporary emergency as request heightened, and the charm of rhino horns rose above borders.

2. **The Rhino Species and Their Shaky Presence**
   Rhinos, having a place with different animal varieties like the Dark, White, Indian, Sumatran, and Javan, have confronted a raising danger to their endurance. Unmistakable in their attributes and territories, every species experiences remarkable difficulties. The dissemination of rhinos traverses Africa and Asia, and the particular weaknesses of every species feature the desperation of custom fitted protection procedures. The steady poaching pressure has driven these great animals to the edge of elimination, requiring worldwide participation to guarantee their proceeded with presence.

3. **Meaning of Rhino Horns in Customary Medication and Social Practices**
   The meaning of rhino horns in conventional medication and social practices stays a main thrust behind their unlawful exchange. Established in age-old convictions, particularly in pieces of Asia, rhino horns are mistakenly seen to have restorative properties, in spite of logical proof going against the norm. Social ceremonies and superficial points of interest further fuel interest, making

a relentless market that rises above worldwide lines and opposes preservation endeavors.

4. **The Misinterpretation Encompassing the Restorative Properties of Rhino Horns**

One of the focal misinterpretations adding to the emergency is the confidence in the restorative properties of rhino horns. Regardless of an absence of logical proof supporting their viability, request endures, propagated by customary healers and unwarranted social convictions. Unraveling this misinterpretation is essential for testing the main driver of the emergency and reshaping public perspectives toward the utilization of rhino horns in conventional medication.

5. **Ascent of Rhino Horn Dealing: Verifiable Setting**

The contemporary rhino horn dealing emergency has developed from confined practices to a refined and exceptionally worthwhile worldwide exchange. Authentic occasions, for example, the inconvenience of global embargoes, have molded the direction of the emergency.

Notwithstanding, the unquenchable interest, combined with the contribution of coordinated criminal organizations, has impelled rhino horn dealing into a remarkable and testing domain. The verifiable setting gives pivotal experiences into the elements that fuel the exchange and the transformations expected for compelling protection.

6. **Factors Filling the Interest for Rhino Horns**

The interest for rhino horns is a complex test impacted by monetary, social, and international variables. Rising abundance, combined with the view of rhino horns as extravagance things and superficial points of interest, increases request. The complex trap of elements adding to this request stretches out past territorial limits, requiring a nuanced and worldwide composed reaction to check the emergency.

7. **Criminal Organizations and Their Contribution**

At the core of the rhino horn dealing emergency lies a refined organization of coordinated wrongdoing. Criminal organizations, with their mind boggling tasks and worldwide reach, exploit administrative escape clauses, degenerate authorities, and influence innovation to coordinate the unlawful exchange. The inclusion of such organizations represents an imposing test to policing and protectionists, requesting creative and cooperative ways to deal with destroy these crook undertakings.

8. **Influence on Rhino Populaces: A Protection Emergency**

Rhino populaces face an existential danger because of the constant poaching for their horns. The effect stretches out past the prompt loss of individual creatures to the destabilization of whole environments. The decrease in rhino numbers disturbs biological equilibriums, influencing biodiversity and the versatility of regular natural surroundings. Protectionists wrestle with the earnest need to address this emergency to forestall irreversible harm to these notorious species and their surroundings.

9. **Insights on Rhino Populace Decline: A Quantitative Point of view**

Measuring the size of the emergency gives an obvious image of the quick decrease in rhino populaces. Factual information uncovers disturbing patterns, for certain species wavering near the very edge of elimination. Provincial varieties in poaching power highlight the requirement for designated mediations. By understanding the quantitative parts of rhino populace decline, policymakers and progressives can fit techniques to address explicit difficulties looked by changed species.

10. **Natural Results of Rhino Poaching**

Past the mathematical decrease in rhino populaces, the environmental results of poaching resonate through biological systems. Rhinos assume a pivotal part as cornerstone species, molding scenes and impacting plant and creature networks.

The expulsion of rhinos disturbs these many-sided environmental communications, prompting flowing impacts that reach out to different species. Looking at these natural repercussions accentuates the earnestness of protecting rhino populaces for the general wellbeing of environments.

In the sections that follow, Past Boundaries: The Worldwide Effect of Rhino Horn Dealing further unwinds the layers of this emergency, investigating endeavors and difficulties in preservation, the human expense of dealing, the ascent of coordinated wrongdoing, and the financial repercussions. By digging into the complexities of the rhino horn dealing emergency, this thorough investigation means to stir aggregate activity to shield the eventual fate of rhinos and save the rich biodiversity of our planet.

B. The global significance of the issue

The emergency of rhino horn dealing rises above geological limits, reverberating internationally as a basic issue that stretches out a long ways past the domains of preservation. This perplexing test holds enormous importance for the whole planet, entwining natural, financial, social, and international aspects. Looking at the worldwide effect of rhino horn dealing uncovers the interconnected web that interfaces the destiny of these notorious animals to more extensive difficulties looked by mankind.

1. **Natural Interconnectedness: Danger to Biodiversity**

At the center of the worldwide importance lies the effect of rhino horn dealing on biodiversity. Rhinos, as cornerstone species, assume a urgent part in forming biological systems. Their particular touching examples impact vegetation, making territories that help different verdure. The pulverization of rhino populaces upsets these fragile natural adjusts, setting off a cascading type of influence that resonates through whole environments. The deficiency of biodiversity reduces the strength of normal living spaces as well as compromises the general soundness of the planet.

2. **Protection as a Worldwide Goal**

The worldwide meaning of rhino horn dealing is highlighted by the basic for global participation in preservation endeavors. Rhinos, possessing districts across Africa and Asia, are dependent upon transnational dangers. Cooperative drives become principal to successfully combatting poaching, destroying criminal organizations, and executing protection systems. The interconnected idea of environments and natural life populaces requires a unified front against the illegal exchange rhino horns, stressing the requirement for shared liability on a worldwide scale.

3. **Financial Consequences: Effect on Feasible Turn of events**

Rhino horn dealing presents monetary difficulties that reach out past the preservation area. Nations with rhino populaces frequently depend on untamed life the travel industry as a critical wellspring of income. The decrease in rhino populaces undermines the travel industry, influencing jobs and monetary maintainability. Adjusting the financial advantages of the travel industry with preservation objectives turns into a fragile condition, featuring the requirement for an all encompassing methodology that shields both normal assets and monetary prosperity.

4. **Social Resonations: Protecting Legacy and Customs**

The interest for rhino horns is well established in social practices, especially in specific Asian social orders. Understanding and addressing these social subtleties are fundamental to controling the interest for rhino horns. Worldwide endeavors should explore the sensitive harmony between regarding social legacy and safeguarding the biodiversity that supports these customs. By cultivating social responsiveness and mindfulness, the worldwide local area can add to reshaping perspectives toward the utilization of rhino horns without forcing outside values.

5. **International Ramifications: Discretion and Global Relations**

Rhino horn dealing has international ramifications, testing political relations and global collaboration. Nations impacted by the exchange should participate in political endeavors to encourage cooperation, share knowledge, and address the main drivers of the emergency. The illegal exchange's worldwide reach requires a planned reaction, and the international meaning of rhino horn dealing with stresses the significance of discretionary arrangements the battle against untamed life wrongdoing.

6. **Security Dangers: Linkages to Coordinated Wrongdoing**

The contribution of coordinated criminal organizations in rhino horn dealing presents security dangers on a worldwide scale. These organizations, frequently participated in different types of illegal exchange and crimes, subvert law and order and posture difficulties to public and worldwide security. The battle against rhino horn dealing converges with more extensive endeavors to battle coordinated wrongdoing, building up the requirement for a multi-layered and cooperative way to deal with address these interconnected difficulties.

7. **Moral and Moral Goals: A Common Obligation**

Past the biological, monetary, and international aspects, the issue of rhino horn dealing summons moral and moral goals that resound universally. The destiny of rhinos represents mankind's stewardship of the normal world and our obligation to safeguard and protect Earth's different species.

The worldwide local area shares an ethical obligation to address the underlying drivers of rhino horn dealing, pushing for moral shopper decisions, supporting protection drives, and encouraging an aggregate obligation to defending the planet's biodiversity.

C. Purpose of the book: Unveiling the interconnectedness and far-reaching consequences

"Past Lines: The Worldwide Effect of Rhino Horn Dealing" is made with a solitary and significant reason — to enlighten the mind boggling snare of interconnectedness encompassing the emergency of rhino horn dealing and to uncover the sweeping outcomes that reach out past the prompt preservation setting. This object is established in a profound obligation to cultivating grasping, mindfulness, and a need to get a move on among perusers, catalyzing an aggregate reaction to resolve this perplexing issue.

1. **Exposing Interconnectedness: Connecting Biological, Social, and Worldwide Real factors**
   The book's essential goal is to expose the interconnectedness that ties rhino horn dealing to environmental, social, and worldwide real factors. By diving into the authentic, social, and environmental components of the emergency, the account looks to show that the destiny of rhinos isn't disengaged yet unpredictably woven into the more extensive texture of our planet. The interconnectedness between the poaching of rhinos, the illegal exchange their horns, and the environmental equilibrium of whole biological systems highlights the desperation for an all encompassing and cooperative methodology.

2. **Environmental String: Exhibiting the Far reaching influence on Biodiversity**
   At its center, the book tries to exhibit the biological string that goes through the emergency. The widespread poaching of rhinos, driven by the interest for their horns, sets off a gradually expanding influence that reaches out a long ways past the prompt loss of individual creatures. By clarifying the flowing outcomes on biodiversity, environments, and the fragile equilibrium of nature, the story begs

perusers to perceive the significant biological stakes and the basic for worldwide protection endeavors.

3. **Social Setting: Unraveling Fantasies and Changing Mentalities**

   A urgent part of the book's motivation is to investigate the social setting that energizes the interest for rhino horns. Customary convictions and practices, especially in specific Asian societies, are examined with a nuanced approach. By unraveling fantasies encompassing the alleged restorative properties of rhino horns, the book expects to cultivate a change in social perspectives. It welcomes perusers to see the value in the rich embroidery of different societies while testing unsafe practices that add to the peril of an animal varieties.

4. **Worldwide Real factors: Stressing Shared Liability and Collaboration**

   "Past Boundaries" endeavors to put forth for its perusers the worldwide real factors of rhino horn dealing. The emergency reaches out past the boundaries of individual countries, requiring aggregate activity on a worldwide scale. The account underlines the common obligation of the worldwide local area in battling the unlawful exchange, destroying criminal organizations, and carrying out viable preservation systems. The interconnectedness of the worldwide re-action is highlighted, encouraging countries to save international contrasts for the protection of a common regular legacy.

5. **Extensive Results: From Security Dangers to Monetary Effect**

   The book fastidiously depicts the expansive results of rhino horn dealing. From security dangers presented by coordinated criminal organizations to the financial effect on networks dependent on natural life the travel industry, the story illustrates the inadvertent blow-back created by the illegal exchange. By interfacing these results to more extensive worldwide difficulties, the book prompts perusers to perceive the desperation of tending to rhino horn dealing as a complex issue with suggestions that broaden well past the domains of preservation.

6. **Catalyzing Activity: From Attention to Support**

Eventually, the reason for "Past Boundaries" is to catalyze activity. The book looks to rouse perusers to move past detached attention to dynamic promotion. By introducing a comprehensive comprehension of the emergency and its interconnected aspects, the story plans to enable people, networks, policymakers, and worldwide bodies to make significant and cooperative strides. Whether it be supporting protection drives, upholding for stricter guidelines, or encouraging moral purchaser decisions, the book welcomes perusers to become partners in the worldwide work to battle rhino horn dealing.

Fundamentally, "Past Lines" tries to be in excess of a story; it is a source of inspiration. By disentangling the layers of intricacy encompassing rhino horn dealing and uncovering its interconnectedness with worldwide real factors, the book means to light an aggregate obligation to shielding the eventual fate of rhinos, protecting biodiversity, and tending to the more extensive difficulties that undermine our common planet. A demonstration of the conviction understanding the profundity of interconnectedness is the most important move towards making practical arrangements that rise above borders and secure a future where rhinos flourish and biological systems thrive.

Chapter 1

The Rhino And Its Horn

The rhinoceros, an eminent and old animal, has long caught the creative mind of individuals all over the planet. Integral to its charm is the rhino's horn, an extraordinary element that holds social, verifiable, and monetary importance. This paper looks to give an exhaustive investigation of the rhino and its horn, disentangling the many-sided layers of fantasy, social practices, and the difficulties looked by these animals in the cutting edge world.

1. **Rhino Species and Dissemination:**
   To comprehend the meaning of the rhino's horn, it's vital for first dig into the different species that make up the rhinoceros family. There are five surviving rhino species: the White Rhino, Dark Rhino, Indian Rhino, Javan Rhino, and Sumatran Rhino. Every species is particular in its attributes, natural surroundings, and preservation status. The dissemination of rhinos ranges across Africa and Asia, with every species adjusted to its particular climate.

2. **Social Meaning of Rhino Horns:**
   Rhino horns hold a well established social importance in different social orders. Frequently viewed as images of solidarity, status, and recuperating, rhino horns have been integrated into customary practices and ceremonies. In certain societies, the horn is accepted to have restorative properties, prompting its utilization in customary medication regardless of an absence of logical proof. Understanding these social convictions is pivotal in tending to the interest for rhino horns and contriving successful preservation procedures.

3. **The Confusion Encompassing Restorative Properties:**
   One of the most persevering through legends related with rhino horns is their alleged restorative properties. Regardless of an absence of logical proof supporting any remedial impacts, interest for rhino horns continues because of extremely old convictions. Investigating the foundations of these misinterpretations is

imperative in making mindfulness and dissipating the legends that drive the unlawful exchange rhino horns.

4. **Authentic Setting of Rhino Horn Exchange:**
The historical backdrop of rhino horn exchange is a mind boggling story entwined with investigation, colonization, and changing worldwide elements. From the verifiable utilization of rhino horns by native networks to the rise of shipping lanes interfacing Africa and Asia, the interest for these valuable members has a long and tangled history. Analyzing this authentic setting gives bits of knowledge into the variables that have energized the unlawful exchange and poaching of rhinos.

5. **Monetary Worth and Poaching:**
The financial worth joined to rhino horns has been a main impetus behind widespread poaching. With the interest for rhino horns continuing in different business sectors, including those determined by conventional medication and the making of fancy things, the illegal exchange has turned into a rewarding undertaking for criminal organizations. The unforgiving truth of poaching undermines individual rhino populaces as well as the delicate environments they occupy.

6. **Protection Endeavors and Difficulties:**
Endeavors to monitor rhino populaces have been met with the two triumphs and difficulties. Different preservation associations and states are effectively engaged with hostile to poaching drives, natural surroundings insurance, and local area commitment programs. Be that as it may, the fight against poaching stays considerable, with challenges including restricted assets, defilement, and the always developing systems utilized by criminal organizations. An investigation of these endeavors gives understanding into the continuous battle to shield these famous animals.

7. **Environmental Outcomes of Rhino Poaching:**
Past the prompt danger to rhino populaces, poaching has significant natural outcomes. Rhinos assume a critical part in forming their biological systems through cycles like seed dispersal and vegetation the executives. The decay of rhino populaces disturbs these biological elements, prompting flowing consequences for different species and the general wellbeing of the environments they occupy.

8. **Local area Association in Protection:**
Connecting with neighborhood networks is urgent to the progress of rhino preservation endeavors. Understanding the financial variables that drive networks to take part in poaching exercises is critical in creating manageable other options. Local area based preservation drives that focus on training, monetary turn of events, and concurrence with untamed life offer a promising way to deal with tending to the underlying drivers of poaching.

9. **Mechanical Developments in Preservation:**
   Innovation has arisen as a strong partner in the battle against rhino poaching. From the utilization of robots and satellite symbolism to screen and safeguard rhino populaces to the advancement of shrewd GPS beacons, mechanical developments give new instruments to progressives. Investigating these progressions reveals insight into how innovation is reshaping the scene of rhino preservation.

10. **Worldwide Coordinated effort for Rhino Preservation:**

Given the transnational idea of rhino horn dealing, worldwide joint effort is fundamental in actually tending to the emergency. Peaceful accords, associations among states, and participation among preservation associations assume a significant part in pooling assets and mastery. Looking at effective models of worldwide cooperation gives bits of knowledge into the possibility to a unified front against the unlawful exchange rhino horns.

1.1 Rhino species and distribution

The rhinoceros, an old and famous species, comprises of five surviving species, each with extraordinary qualities and transformations. The variety in rhino species is essential to understanding their perplexing dispersion designs and the difficulties they face. This paper gives a thorough investigation of the different rhino species, their conveyance across landmasses, and the preservation endeavors pointed toward guaranteeing their endurance.

1. **The White Rhino (Ceratotherium simum):**
   The White Rhino, with its square-molded mouth adjusted for touching, is one of the biggest land well evolved creatures. This species contains two subspecies: the Southern White Rhino and the basically jeopardized Northern White Rhino. By and large, the Southern White Rhino has been more various, fundamentally found in Southern Africa, especially in nations like South Africa, Namibia, Zimbabwe, and Kenya. The more restricted Northern White Rhino populace, notwithstanding, was once dispersed across Uganda, Sudan, Chad, and the Majority rule Republic of the Congo.

2. **The Dark Rhino (Diceros bicornis):**
   Rather than the White Rhino, the Dark Rhino is portrayed by its snared upper lip, which is prehensile and adjusted for getting a handle on leaves and twigs. The Dark Rhino is additionally partitioned into four subspecies: the South-focal, South-western, East African, and West African Dark Rhinos. Generally circulated across a wide reach in Africa, from savannas to thick timberlands, Dark Rhinos have confronted extreme populace declines because of poaching. Preservation endeavors have zeroed in on safeguarding their leftover populaces in nations like Namibia, Zimbabwe, and South Africa.

3. **The Indian Rhino (Rhinoceros unicornis):**
   The Indian Rhino, otherwise called the one-horned rhinoceros, is local to the Indian subcontinent. Found in India and Nepal, this species favors the prairies and marshes of the Terai-Duar savanna and floodplain biological systems. With a solitary horn and thick, reinforcement like skin, Indian Rhinos have been a preservation example of overcoming adversity lately, with purposeful endeavors prompting populace expansions in safeguarded regions like Kaziranga Public Park in India.

4. **The Javan Rhino (Rhinoceros sondaicus):**
   The Javan Rhino is one of the most extraordinary rhino species, with a populace focused on the island of Java in Indonesia. By and large, they additionally possessed pieces of Southeast Asia, yet living space misfortune and poaching have limited their reach. The Ujung Kulon Public Park in Java stays the last fortress for this fundamentally jeopardized species. Preservation drives plan to shield their territory and guarantee the endurance of this novel rhino.

5. **The Sumatran Rhino (Dicerorhinus sumatrensis):**
   The littlest and hairiest of the rhino species, the Sumatran Rhino is local to Sumatra and Borneo. By and large, they had a greater reach across Southeast Asia, however territory misfortune and poaching have fundamentally diminished their numbers. Preservation endeavors center around safeguarding remaining populaces in Sumatra, where they occupy thick timberlands. The hostage rearing system likewise assumes a urgent part in the preservation of this fundamentally imperiled species.

6. **Conveyance Examples and Environment Inclinations:**
   Rhino species show assorted circulation examples and natural surroundings inclinations in view of their developmental transformations. While White Rhinos flourish in fields and savannas, Dark Rhinos have adjusted to a more extensive scope of environments, from meadows to thick backwoods. The Indian Rhino's inclination for marshy prairies and the Javan and Sumatran Rhinos' partiality for thick backwoods feature the specific environments essential for their endurance.

7. **Dangers to Rhino Species:**
   Notwithstanding their versatility, rhino species face various dangers, fundamentally determined by human exercises. Natural surroundings misfortune because of agribusiness and urbanization, combined with the unlawful untamed life exchange, presents huge difficulties.
   Poaching for rhino horns, driven by conventional convictions and high market interest, stays a basic danger to their endurance. Environmental change and related natural changes further compound the difficulties looked by rhino populaces.

8. **Protection Systems:**
   Protection endeavors for rhino species include a diverse methodology, tending

to both prompt dangers and long haul maintainability. Safeguarded regions, for example, public stops and holds, assume a vital part in giving safe territories to rhinos. Hostile to poaching drives, local area contribution, and worldwide joint efforts intend to control unlawful natural life exchange and shield rhinos from poachers.

9. **Examples of overcoming adversity and Difficulties:**
   Some rhino protection drives have yielded positive outcomes, showing the viability of deliberate endeavors. Fruitful rearing projects, territory reclamation, and local area commitment have added to populace expansions in specific regions. Notwithstanding, challenges continue, including restricted assets, political shakiness, and the continuous interest for rhino horns. The new flood in mechanical developments, like high level observing frameworks and DNA examination, gives new apparatuses to address these difficulties.

10. **Future Viewpoint:**

The eventual fate of rhino species depends on the worldwide obligation to protection and feasible practices. Proceeded with endeavors to safeguard natural surroundings, battle poaching, and draw in neighborhood networks are fundamental. Worldwide participation and inventive methodologies, combined with public mindfulness and instruction, can add to the safeguarding of these glorious animals for people in the future.

1.2 Significance of rhino horns in traditional medicine and cultural practices

The rhinoceros, with its unmistakable horn, holds an extraordinary spot in the social and conventional acts of different social orders. The importance ascribed to rhino horns has profound authentic roots, entwined with convictions in customary medication, social ceremonies, and emblematic portrayals. This article investigates the intricate connection between rhino horns and human societies, digging into the legends, convictions, and preservation challenges related with the interest for these valuable extremities.

1. **Authentic Foundations of Rhino Horn Use:**
   The utilization of rhino horns in conventional medication and social practices goes back hundreds of years, with verifiable records reporting their presence in old Asian social orders. Rhino horns were accepted to have restorative properties and were viewed as important fixings in conventional cures. Also, the hardness and solidness of rhino horns made them appealing materials for creating elaborate things, further expanding their social importance.

2. **Rhino Horns in Conventional Medication:**
   One of the essential purposes behind the persevering interest for rhino horns is their apparent restorative properties. Customary medication frameworks in pieces of Asia, especially in nations like China and Vietnam, have long loved

rhino horns for their alleged recuperating skills. Convictions in the horn's strength to fix different illnesses, from fever to malignant growth, have added to the continuous interest and filled the unlawful exchange rhino horns.

3. **Social Imagery and Status:**
Past therapeutic use, rhino horns have emblematic importance in many societies. The rhinoceros, as a strong and tough animal, represents strength and perseverance. Claiming or showing rhino horn antiquities has been related with glory and status in specific social orders, where these things might act as images of abundance, power, or otherworldly importance. Understanding the social imagery connected to rhino horns is pivotal in tending to the intricacies of interest and formulating compelling preservation methodologies.

4. **Customary Practices and Ceremonies:**
Notwithstanding therapeutic and emblematic purposes, rhino horns are frequently integrated into conventional practices and ceremonies. These customs can go from strict services to soul changing experiences. For certain networks, the utilization of rhino horns is profoundly imbued in social customs, making it trying to move discernments and ways of behaving. Perceiving the social setting of rhino horn use is fundamental for creating protection moves toward that regard and draw in with neighborhood networks.

5. **Legends and Misguided judgments:**
The getting through interest for rhino horns is propagated by fantasies and confusions encompassing their viability. Notwithstanding an absence of logical proof supporting the restorative properties of rhino horns, profoundly imbued convictions endure. Legends encompassing the healing powers of rhino horns add to the difficulties looked by traditionalists in modifying buyer conduct and decreasing the interest for these valuable members.

6. **Protection Difficulties:**
The social and customary meaning of rhino horns presents imposing difficulties to preservation endeavors. The unlawful exchange rhino horns, driven by request from customary medication markets and social inclinations, represents an immediate danger to rhino populaces around the world. The high market worth of rhino horns makes impetuses for poaching, prompting a decrease in rhino numbers and undermining the endurance of specific species. Preservationists face the fragile undertaking of tending to social practices while upholding for the assurance of these imperiled creatures.

7. **Influence on Rhino Populaces:**
The tireless interest for rhino horns has negatively affected rhino populaces internationally. Poaching, driven by the rewarding exchange, has prompted a critical decrease in rhino numbers, driving a few animal categories to the edge of eradication. The effect isn't just on individual rhinos yet in addition on the more extensive environments they possess. Understanding the immediate connection

between's social practices, interest for rhino horns, and populace decline is pivotal for executing compelling preservation systems.

8. **Against Poaching and Implementation Endeavors:**
Progressives and states have carried out enemy of poaching and requirement measures to battle the unlawful exchange rhino horns. These endeavors include the organization of officers, the utilization of trend setting innovation for checking and reconnaissance, and worldwide coordinated effort to destroy criminal organizations. In any case, the social and conventional underlying foundations of rhino horn request present continuous difficulties to requirement, requiring a multi-layered approach that tends to the main drivers of the issue.

9. **Schooling and Mindfulness Drives:**
Schooling and mindfulness crusades assume a fundamental part in tending to the social meaning of rhino horns. These drives mean to scatter legends, advance logical comprehension, and draw in with networks to encourage a feeling of obligation toward preservation. By giving precise data and featuring the environmental effect of the exchange, schooling endeavors look to reshape perspectives and diminish interest for rhino horns.

10. **Local area Commitment and Reasonable Other options:**
Drawing in with nearby networks is a basic part of protection techniques. Perceiving the social meaning of rhino horns, endeavors ought to zero in on furnishing manageable options that line up with nearby customs.
Local area based protection drives, which include cooperation between protection associations and nearby inhabitants, mean to work out some kind of harmony between social practices and the conservation of rhino populaces.

11. **Legitimate Systems and Worldwide Participation:**

Tending to the social interest for rhino horns requires neighborhood drives as well as a worldwide methodology. Reinforcing legitimate systems, upgrading punishments for unlawful exchange, and encouraging worldwide participation are fundamental stages in checking the interest for rhino horns. Conciliatory endeavors and associations between nations can work with the sharing of knowledge, requirement methodologies, and best practices in preservation.

1.3 The misconception surrounding the medicinal properties of rhino horns

The confidence in the restorative properties of rhino horns has continued for quite a long time, well established in social practices and conventional medication. This paper embraces an exhaustive investigation of the misinterpretations encompassing the alleged mending powers of rhino horns. We dive into the authentic setting, social importance, natural results, and preservation challenges related with the persevering interest for rhino horns in customary medication.

1. **Authentic Foundations of Restorative Convictions:**
   The authentic foundations of the faith in rhino horn's restorative properties follow back to antiquated times, especially in specific Asian societies. Customary Chinese Medication (TCM) and other conventional mending frameworks have ascribed different medical advantages to rhino horns, going from fever decrease to the therapy of additional serious sicknesses. Understanding the verifiable setting is critical in unwinding the getting through nature of these convictions and their effect on rhino populaces.

2. **Conventional Chinese Medication and Rhino Horns:**
   Inside Conventional Chinese Medication, rhino horns have been generally recommended for different circumstances. The idea of "cooling" properties credited to rhino horns has prompted their utilization in treating high fevers and fiery circumstances. Regardless of lacking logical proof, the confidence in the viability of rhino horns has continued, encouraging a critical interest and driving the unlawful exchange these valuable members.

3. **Social Importance and Imagery:**
   The social meaning of rhino horns reaches out past their apparent restorative properties. Rhinos themselves hold emblematic worth in different societies, addressing strength, versatility, and power. The fuse of rhino horns into social practices, customs, and images muddles the endeavors to change insights and decrease the interest for these famous animals' horns.

4. **Logical Viewpoint on Rhino Horns:**
   From a logical outlook, rhino horns are made out of keratin, a similar protein tracked down in human hair and nails. They have no exceptional restorative properties. Notwithstanding the shortfall of observational proof supporting their viability, the relentless confidence in the mending powers of rhino horns keeps on driving interest, sustaining the danger to rhino populaces.

5. **Protection Effect:**
   The misinterpretation encompassing the restorative properties of rhino horns has significant ramifications for rhino populaces and their biological systems. The unlawful exchange driven by social convictions brings about far and wide poaching, compromising the endurance of rhino species around the world. The biological outcomes stretch out past the immediate effect on rhinos, influencing the perplexing equilibrium of their natural surroundings and adding to biodiversity misfortune.

6. **Rhino Populace Decline:**
   The interest for rhino horns has powered a staggering expansion in poaching exercises, prompting an uncommon decrease in rhino populaces. Species, for example, the African Dark Rhino and the Sumatran Rhino have confronted extreme populace decreases, driving a subspecies to the edge of eradication. The

interconnectedness between social convictions and the decay of rhino populaces highlights the criticalness of tending to these misguided judgments.

7. **Legitimate Systems and Requirement:**
Legislatures and protection associations have carried out legitimate structures and authorization measures to check the unlawful exchange rhino horns. In any case, the determination of social convictions presents difficulties to successful implementation. Fortifying punishments, improving cross-line coordinated effort, and destroying criminal organizations are fundamental parts of tending to the illegal exchange and safeguarding rhino populaces.

8. **Social Awareness in Preservation:**
Perceiving the social awareness encompassing rhino horn use is significant in planning protection procedures that are both viable and deferential. Protectionists should explore the sensitive harmony between advancing mindfulness about the environmental effect of the exchange and regarding social practices. Social responsiveness can open roads for discourse and cooperation with networks, cultivating a common obligation to rhino preservation.

9. **Public Mindfulness and Schooling:**
Public mindfulness missions and schooling drives assume a urgent part in testing and changing misinterpretations encompassing the restorative properties of rhino horns. These endeavors mean to give precise data, scatter fantasies, and cultivate a comprehension of the natural significance of rhinos. By drawing in with people in general, especially in locales where convictions are profoundly imbued, preservationists can lay the preparation for attitudinal movements.

10. **Elective Medications and Substitutes:**
Investigating elective medications and substitutes is a basic part of tending to the interest for rhino horns. Examination into manageable, socially satisfactory choices can furnish reasonable choices that line up with conventional recuperating rehearses without hurting rhino populaces. Cooperative endeavors between moderates, analysts, and conventional medication experts can drive the turn of events and reception of choices.

11. **Worldwide Cooperation and Strategy:**
Given the worldwide idea of the unlawful exchange, global cooperation and discretionary endeavors are fundamental in tending to the misinterpretation encompassing rhino horns. Tact can work with discourse between nations, empowering the sharing of information, assets, and techniques to battle the unlawful exchange. Worldwide drives can cultivate a unified front against the social misinterpretations driving the interest for rhino horns.

12. **Mechanical Developments in Preservation:**
Mechanical progressions offer new roads for moderates to address the misinterpretation encompassing rhino horns. From cutting edge observing frameworks to DNA examination, innovation can support following and forestalling

poaching exercises. Imaginative methodologies, for example, the utilization of fake rhino horns to befuddle unlawful business sectors, feature the potential for innovation to disturb the unlawful exchange while regarding social awarenesses.

13. **Local area Association and Strengthening:**
Connecting with neighborhood networks in protection endeavors is necessary to tending to the misinterpretation encompassing rhino horns. Local area inclusion can go from schooling projects to reasonable improvement drives that enable neighborhood inhabitants financially. By encouraging a feeling of stewardship and responsibility for populaces, networks become dynamic members in preservation as opposed to accidental supporters of the unlawful exchange.

14. **Examples of overcoming adversity and Illustrations Learned:**
Looking at examples of overcoming adversity in protection gives important experiences into compelling systems for tending to the confusion encompassing rhino horns. Contextual investigations where social perspectives have moved, and protection endeavors have yielded positive outcomes offer illustrations for scaling effective methodologies and fitting intercessions to assorted social settings.

15. **Future Points of view and Difficulties:**

The fate of rhino preservation depends on the aggregate endeavors to challenge and change the confusion encompassing the restorative properties of rhino horns. While progress has been made, challenges endure, including profoundly instilled social convictions, continuous interest, and the requirement for supported worldwide cooperation. Future viewpoints should focus on versatile procedures, social awareness, and all encompassing methodologies that address the underlying drivers of the misinterpretation.

Chapter 2

Rise Of Rhino Horn Trafficking

The unlawful exchange rhino horns has flooded as of late, representing a serious danger to rhino populaces around the world. This paper embraces a far reaching investigation of the ascent of rhino horn dealing, looking at its verifiable setting, the variables driving the interest, the lawbreaker networks included, natural outcomes, and the worldwide reactions pointed toward controling this illegal exchange.

1. **Verifiable Setting of Rhino Horn Exchange:**
   The historical backdrop of rhino horn exchange can be followed back hundreds of years, with verifiable records reporting its utilization in different societies and social orders. While rhino horns have been generally esteemed for their apparent restorative properties and representative importance, the cutting edge flood in dealing addresses a later and disturbing pattern. Understanding the verifiable setting gives bits of knowledge into the advancement of this illegal exchange and its effect on rhino populaces.

2. **Factors Filling the Interest for Rhino Horns:**
   A few interconnected factors add to the ascent popular for rhino horns. Conventional medication rehearses, especially in specific Asian societies, have propagated the faith in the recuperating properties of rhino horns. The representative meaning of rhino horns in status and riches, joined with the worldwide market for elaborate things, has spurred a worthwhile interest. Financial differences, debasement, and powerless policing fuel the issue, establishing a helpful climate for criminal organizations to take advantage of.

3. **Criminal Organizations Engaged with Rhino Horn Dealing:**
   The unlawful exchange rhino horns is worked with by complex crook networks working on a worldwide scale. These organizations participate in poaching, transportation, and conveyance of rhino horns, frequently utilizing profoundly coordinated and secret techniques. The contribution of coordinated wrongdoing, with connections to other unlawful exercises, for example, tax evasion

and debasement, makes rhino horn dealing an intricate and provoking issue to address.

4. **Poaching: The Quick Danger to Rhinos:**
Poaching is the most immediate and prompt danger to rhino populaces. Energized by the interest for rhino horns, poachers utilize progressively refined methods, including night vision hardware and powerful weaponry.
The effect on rhino populaces is crushing, with individual creatures focused on for their horns, frequently prompting fatalities and a decrease in conceptive rates. Hostile to poaching endeavors, while basic, face various difficulties in fighting efficient and vigorously equipped poaching organizations.

5. **Natural Outcomes of Rhino Poaching:**
The natural outcomes of rhino poaching reach out past the prompt danger to individual creatures. Rhinos assume a fundamental part in forming their biological systems through cycles like seed dispersal, vegetation the board, and touching examples. The decrease in rhino populaces disturbs these environmental elements, prompting flowing consequences for different species and the general strength of the biological systems they possess.

6. **Financial Consequences of Rhino Horn Dealing:**
The monetary effect of rhino horn dealing is huge and stretches out past the prompt districts impacted. Nations with rhino populaces frequently face monetary misfortunes because of decreased the travel industry, a decrease in environment administrations, and the expenses related with hostile to poaching endeavors. Furthermore, the contribution of nearby networks in poaching exercises, driven by monetary distress, features the complex financial repercussions of the unlawful exchange.

7. **Defilement and Frail Policing:**
Defilement and frail policing significant difficulties in fighting rhino horn dealing. The contribution of authorities in the unlawful exchange chain, whether through pay off or conspiracy, hampers endeavors to implement existing guidelines. Fortifying legitimate systems, upgrading punishments, and further developing policing are fundamental parts of tending to the main drivers of debasement in the exchange.

8. **Worldwide Financial Ramifications of Unlawful Untamed life Exchange:**
The unlawful natural life exchange, including rhino horn dealing, has more extensive worldwide monetary ramifications. The interconnected idea of the worldwide economy implies that the results of untamed life dealing stretch out past the nations straightforwardly involved. The deficiency of biodiversity, disturbances to biological systems, and the expected spread of zoonotic illnesses highlight the requirement for global cooperation to address the main drivers of the unlawful exchange.

9. **Global Reaction to Rhino Horn Dealing:**

The global local area has perceived the seriousness of the rhino horn dealing emergency and has answered with different measures. Peaceful accords, for example, the Show on Global Exchange Jeopardized Types of Wild Fauna and Vegetation (Refers to), expect to direct and confine the exchange imperiled species, including rhinos. Cooperative endeavors between nations, NGOs, and protection associations are in progress to share knowledge, coordinate enemy of poaching drives, and bring issues to light about the outcomes of the unlawful exchange.

10. **Lawful Systems and Hostile to Dealing Regulation:**

Fortifying legitimate systems and against dealing regulation is urgent in tending to the ascent of rhino horn dealing. Nations with rhino populaces are asked to establish and uphold rigid regulations that force serious punishments for association in the unlawful exchange. Worldwide participation is crucial for close lawful escape clauses, fit guidelines, and work with the removal of people associated with rhino horn dealing across borders.

11. **Mechanical Advancements in Enemy of Poaching Endeavors:**

Innovation assumes a urgent part in present day enemy of poaching endeavors. Progressions, for example, drone reconnaissance, GPS following, and sensor innovations have upgraded the capacities of officers and policing. Shrewd observing frameworks empower constant following of rhino populaces, forestalling poaching occurrences and giving pivotal information to preservation drives. The coordination of innovation into hostile to poaching methodologies grandstands the potential for development in the battle against rhino horn dealing.

12. **Local area Based Preservation Drives:**

Connecting with neighborhood networks in preservation endeavors is a fundamental technique in tending to the main drivers of rhino horn dealing. Local area based drives include coordinated effort between protection associations and nearby inhabitants to elevate reasonable options in contrast to poaching. These drives might incorporate training programs, monetary improvement ventures, and endeavors to cultivate a deep satisfaction and stewardship over nearby untamed life.

13. **Innovative Techniques to Decrease Interest:**

Tending to the interest for rhino horns requires inventive methodologies that target buyer conduct. Mindfulness crusades, both locally and globally, can assist with dissipating legends encompassing the restorative properties of rhino horns. Drawing in with powerful figures, like superstars and people of note, can enhance protection messages.

Imaginative methodologies, for example, the utilization of computer generated reality encounters, narrating, and social trade programs, intend to move discernments and diminish the interest for rhino horns.

14. **Examples of overcoming adversity and Illustrations Learned:**
    Looking at examples of overcoming adversity in the battle against rhino horn dealing gives important experiences into viable techniques and illustrations learned. Contextual analyses where protection endeavors have brought about populace recuperation, diminished poaching episodes, or changed buyer conduct offer direction for future drives. Sharing examples of overcoming adversity encourages a cooperative soul among nations and associations making progress toward a shared objective.

15. **Future Standpoint and Difficulties:**

The future standpoint for rhino horn dealing stays complex, with progressing difficulties and vulnerabilities. The steadiness of interest, combined with developing strategies utilized by criminal organizations, presents progressing dangers to rhino populaces. The job of environmental change, living space misfortune, and international variables adds intricacy to the protection scene. Tending to these difficulties requires versatile systems, continuous examination, and supported global coordinated effort.

2.1 Historical context of rhino horn trade

The exchange rhino horns has a long and complex history profoundly entwined with social convictions, customary medication, and monetary interests. This exposition plans to investigate the verifiable setting of rhino horn exchange, following its beginnings from antiquated practices to the current day. Understanding this verifiable background is urgent for unwinding the intricacies of the current difficulties confronting rhino populaces and conceiving compelling preservation procedures.

1. **Antiquated Customs and Convictions:**
   The utilization of rhino horns can be followed back to antiquated developments where they held representative and restorative importance. In different societies across Africa and Asia, rhino horns were adored for their apparent supernatural properties. Verifiable records show that rhino horns were used in customs, services, and as brightening relics. The emblematic portrayal of solidarity and power related with rhinos added to their venerated status in old social orders.

2. **Conventional Medication Practices:**
   The foundations of rhino horn exchange expand profoundly into customary medication rehearses, especially in Asian societies. Customary Chinese Medication (TCM) has generally recommended rhino horns for different illnesses, going from fevers to seizures. The faith in the recuperating properties of rhino horns persevered over hundreds of years and added to the interest that at last filled the exchange. The incorporation of rhino horns into customary medication was not restricted to China; it reached out to different pieces of Asia, sustaining the interest for these valued wares.

3. **Fancy and Superficial point of interest:**

   Past restorative use, rhino horns acquired prevalence as elaborate things and images of status. The hardness and sturdiness of rhino horns made them appealing materials for creating mind boggling carvings, gems, and stately items. In specific societies, the ownership of rhino horn curios turned into a superficial point of interest, connoting riches, influence, and social standing. The tasteful allure of rhino horns additionally elevated their attractiveness in imaginative and fancy settings.

4. **Shipping lanes and Worldwide Investigation:**

   The rise of worldwide shipping lanes during the period of investigation further filled the interest for outlandish and important wares, including rhino horns. European wayfarers and brokers looked to fulfill the developing hunger for uncommon and extraordinary things, prompting expanded exchange rhino horns between landmasses. The worldwide trade of products worked with the dispersal of rhino horns, growing their market reach and adding to their commercialization.

5. **Frontier Double-dealing and Decline:**

   Frontier powers, as they continued looking for financial abuse and intriguing merchandise, altogether added to the decay of rhino populaces. The European interest for rhino horns, combined with the presentation of guns, increased hunting and poaching exercises. The precise double-dealing of normal assets during the pilgrim time devastatingly affected rhino populaces, driving specific species to the edge of elimination in unambiguous locales.

6. **Moving Social Practices:**

   As social orders went through social changes and embraced present day rehearses, the meaning of rhino horns in customary medication and ceremonies started to melt away in certain areas. In any case, the tirelessness of convictions and practices in specific networks, combined with the development of new monetary elements, kept on driving interest for rhino horns. The moving social scene and advancing business sector elements introduced the two difficulties and amazing open doors for rhino protection.

7. **Development of Rhino Horn as a Product:**

   In the last 50% of the twentieth 100 years, rhino horn changed from a socially critical thing to a ware driven by worldwide exchange. The monetary worth connected to rhino horns, especially in the unlawful market, turned into a strong impetus for poaching. Rhino populaces, currently helpless because of verifiable double-dealing, confronted a restored and strengthened danger as criminal organizations exploited the rewarding exchange rhino horns.

8. **Lawful Exchange and Administrative Reactions:**

   Endeavors to control the exchange rhino horns came to fruition in the last option part of the twentieth hundred years. The Show on Global Exchange

Jeopardized Types of Wild Fauna and Vegetation (Refers to), laid out in 1973, assumed a significant part in managing and confining the worldwide exchange of imperiled species, including rhinos. Refers to carried out measures to control the exchange rhino horns and advance preservation endeavors.

9. **Rhino Protection Drives:**
Perceiving the criticalness of protecting rhino populaces, preservation drives picked up speed in the last option part of the twentieth 100 years. Public parks, stores, and preservation associations teamed up to safeguard rhino environments and carry out enemy of poaching measures. The center moved towards local area commitment, training, and maintainable advancement to address the underlying drivers of poaching and exchange.

10. **The Ascent of Unlawful Exchange and Poaching:**
Regardless of administrative measures and preservation endeavors, the last option part of the twentieth hundred years and the mid 21st century saw a resurgence in rhino horn dealing. The unlawful exchange rhino horns, driven by request in Asian business sectors and worked with by refined criminal organizations, represented a restored danger to rhino populaces. Poaching episodes raised, and the worth of rhino horns in the unlawful market arrived at exceptional levels.

11. **Market Elements and Monetary Motivators:**
The ascent of rhino horn dealing can be ascribed to advancing business sector elements and financial motivators. The interest for rhino horns continued because of social convictions, status imagery, and the off track faith in their restorative properties. Financial variables, including neediness, restricted elective vocations, and defilement, added to the contribution of neighborhood networks in poaching exercises.
The high market worth of rhino horns made financial motivators for criminal organizations to take advantage of weak populaces and fuel the unlawful exchange.

12. **Innovation and Globalization:**
Progressions in innovation and expanded globalization assumed a double part in the ascent of rhino horn dealing. While innovation worked with preservation endeavors, it additionally gave new roads to criminal organizations to work. The web and online entertainment stages became stages for unlawful natural life exchange, empowering dealers to worldwide interface with purchasers. The simplicity of correspondence and transportation worked with the quick development of rhino horns across borders, convoluting implementation endeavors.

13. **Social Awareness and Protection Difficulties:**
The industriousness of social convictions encompassing rhino horns represents a huge test to protection endeavors. Adjusting the requirement for social responsiveness with the basic to safeguard rhino populaces requires nuanced

techniques. Traditionalists and policymakers should explore the intricacies of social practices, draw in with neighborhood networks, and cultivate understanding to carry out powerful and manageable arrangements.

14. **Current Worldwide Preservation Procedures:**

Even with the raising rhino horn dealing emergency, current worldwide protection systems are multi-layered. They include a mix of policing, commitment, mechanical development, and worldwide cooperation. Against poaching units, furnished with trend setting innovation, watch safeguarded regions, and participate in knowledge drove activities. Local area based protection drives expect to address the financial elements driving poaching, while strategic endeavors work with participation among nations to battle transnational crook organizations.

15. **Future Possibilities and Protection Difficulties:**

What's to come possibilities for rhino horn exchange and preservation are unsure, with various difficulties not too far off. The steadiness of interest, the versatility of criminal organizations, and the interconnected idea of worldwide exchange keep on presenting dangers to rhino populaces. Environmental change, living space misfortune, and international factors further confuse preservation endeavors. The way ahead requires imaginative methodologies, supported global coordinated effort, and a guarantee to tending to the underlying drivers of rhino horn dealing.

2.2 Factors fueling the demand for rhino horns

The interest for rhino horns stays a basic driver behind the tenacious danger to rhino populaces around the world. This article means to dive into the complex factors that fuel the interest for rhino horns, analyzing social convictions, customary medication rehearses, financial drivers, and worldwide market elements. Understanding these elements is fundamental for concocting viable protection procedures that address the main drivers of rhino horn interest.

1. **Social Importance and Imagery:**

The social meaning of rhino horns has profound verifiable roots, assuming a focal part in different social orders' convictions and practices. Rhino horns have been loved for a really long time, representing strength, power, and versatility. The imagery appended to rhino horns reaches out past their functional use, adding to their allure in social settings. Understanding the complicated snare of social convictions encompassing rhino horns is principal to tending to the interest at its center.

2. **Conventional Medication Practices:**

One of the essential drivers of rhino horn request is its apparent restorative properties in customary medication rehearses, especially in specific Asian societies. Customary Chinese Medication (TCM) has generally recommended rhino horns for a scope of infirmities, from fever to spasms. In spite of the absence of logical proof supporting these cases, the well established confidence in the healing powers of rhino horns keeps on filling interest, propagating a pattern of poaching and exchange.

3. **Status Imagery and Riches:**
Rhino horns have become images of status and abundance in specific societies, adding a financial aspect to their interest. The ownership of rhino horn curios, whether as carvings or gems, means esteem and wealth. This status imagery increases the interest for rhino horns, making a market driven by social convictions as well as by financial yearnings and the longing for social acknowledgment.

4. **Fancy and Ornamental Use:**
The elaborate allure of rhino horns has added to their interest in the worldwide market. The extraordinary properties of rhino horns, including their hardness and perplexing grain designs, make them helpful materials for creating fancy things. Carvings, figures, and other beautiful pieces produced using rhino horns get excessive costs in the unlawful market, further boosting poaching and dealing exercises.

5. **Customary Ceremonies and Functions:**
Rhino horns are necessary to specific customary customs and services, adding one more layer to their social importance. In certain networks, rhino horns assume a part in strict services, transitional experiences, or as contributions to otherworldly elements. The coordination of rhino horns into these customs extends their social worth, making it trying to separate the interest from imbued conventional practices.

6. **Monetary Differences and Neediness:**
Financial elements, especially destitution, contribute altogether to the interest for rhino horns. In districts where networks battle with monetary difficulties, the draw of fast monetary profits from partaking in poaching exercises is significant. The financial variations between metropolitan focuses and provincial regions, where rhino populaces frequently live, make conditions helpful for unlawful untamed life exchange for of monetary endurance.

7. **Restricted Elective Jobs:**
The absence of suitable elective jobs for networks dwelling close to rhino environments fuels the dependence on rhino poaching as a type of revenue. Protection endeavors should address the financial elements that drive people to partake in criminal operations. Creating manageable elective occupations, for example, ecotourism drives or local area based protection projects, is vital for diminishing the financial motivations behind rhino horn interest.

8. **Defilement in Administrative Structures:**
Defilement inside administrative structures and policing intensifies the difficulties of fighting rhino horn interest. The association of degenerate authorities in the unlawful exchange chain works with poaching and dealing activities,

sabotaging preservation endeavors. Reinforcing administrative systems, improving straightforwardness, and tending to defilement at all levels are fundamental parts of moderating the interest for rhino horns.

9. **Powerless Policing Insufficient Punishments:**

   In locales where rhino poaching is pervasive, feeble policing lacking punishments add to the interest for rhino horns. Poachers frequently work without any potential repercussions because of remiss requirement measures and permissive punishments. Reinforcing legitimate systems, expanding punishments for poaching and dealing offenses, and improving policing are basic moves toward tending to the interest at its source.

10. **Worldwide Market Elements:**

    The worldwide market elements for natural life items, including rhino horns, assume a critical part in energizing interest. The interconnectedness of the worldwide economy empowers the fast development of unlawful natural life items across borders. The interest for outlandish and uncommon things in worldwide business sectors, driven by authorities and purchasers looking for superficial points of interest, enhances the financial motivations for poaching and dealing.

11. **Absence of Mindfulness and Training:**

    An absence of mindfulness and training in regards to the natural effect of rhino horn exchange adds to the propagation of interest. In certain areas, shoppers may not be completely educated about the outcomes regarding their buying decisions. Schooling efforts that underline the biological significance of rhinos and scatter fantasies encompassing the restorative properties of rhino horns are vital for reshaping shopper conduct.

12. **Tireless Fantasies and Confusions:**

    Legends and confusions encompassing the restorative properties of rhino horns continue regardless of an absence of logical proof. The propagation of these legends through social customs and unconfirmed cases in customary medication energizes the interest for rhino horns. Tending to these misguided judgments requires designated instructive endeavors and commitment with networks to advance a more educated understanding regarding the natural job of rhinos.

13. **Absence of Choices in Conventional Medication:**

    In locales where rhino horn use is profoundly imbued in conventional medication, the absence of OK choices adds to the continuous interest. Endeavors to create and advance socially satisfactory substitutes for rhino horns in conventional medication rehearses are fundamental. Cooperative drives including conventional medication specialists, scientists, and networks can investigate and underwrite maintainable options that line up with social practices.

14. **Natural life Wrongdoing as a Coordinated Endeavor:**

    The commercialization of rhino horn exchange has changed it into a profoundly coordinated and rewarding venture. Criminal organizations work with accuracy, using cutting edge innovation, transportation organizations, and monetary frameworks to work with the unlawful exchange. Understanding the coordinated idea of natural life wrongdoing is essential for contriving implementation methodologies that disturb these organizations and lessen the financial motivations driving the interest.

15. **Absence of Global Collaboration:**

The absence of hearty worldwide participation hampers endeavors to address the worldwide interest for rhino horns. Untamed life dealing is a transnational issue that requires cooperative arrangements. Reinforcing global organizations, sharing knowledge, and fitting administrative systems are fundamental stages in controling the interest for rhino horns and destroying the lawbreaker networks included.

2.3 Criminal networks and their involvement

The unlawful exchange rhino horns isn't simply a result of inconsistent poaching episodes; it is a complex and exceptionally coordinated criminal undertaking. This complete paper plans to dig into the unpredictable trap of criminal organizations engaged with rhino horn dealing. From the complexities of their tasks to the worldwide reach of their organizations, understanding the usual methodology of these criminal substances is pivotal for conceiving powerful techniques to battle the unlawful exchange and safeguard jeopardized rhino populaces.

1. **The Development of Rhino Horn Dealing Organizations:**
   The contribution of criminal organizations in rhino horn dealing has developed over the long haul, reflecting changes in worldwide market elements, mechanical progressions, and policing. Understanding this advancement gives bits of knowledge into the versatile idea of these criminal elements and the difficulties looked by traditionalists and experts in combatting their illegal exercises.

2. **The Globalization of Natural life Wrongdoing:**
   The globalization of the unlawful natural life exchange, including rhino horn dealing, has changed it into a transnational criminal endeavor. Criminal organizations influence worldwide associations, taking advantage of administrative holes and contrasting policing across nations. The interconnected idea of the worldwide economy works with the development of rhino horns across borders, making difficulties for specialists endeavoring to destroy these organizations.

3. **Coordinated Wrongdoing and Rhino Poaching:**
   Rhino poaching, the underlying connection in the crook organization's chain, has become progressively coordinated. Poachers, when individual entertainers, presently frequently work as a component of bigger lawbreaker organizations. The utilization of cutting edge weaponry, night vision hardware, and complex following techniques exhibits the professionalization of poaching exercises.

Understanding the coordinated idea of poaching is fundamental for executing viable enemy of poaching measures.

4. **Funding the Unlawful Exchange:**

   The funding of rhino horn dealing includes complex monetary exchanges and tax evasion plans. Criminal organizations exploit worldwide monetary frameworks, making it provoking for specialists to follow and prohibit unlawful assets. Researching the monetary parts of the exchange is critical for destroying these organizations, upsetting their tasks, and removing the subsidizing that energizes poaching and dealing exercises.

5. **Defilement and Complicity:**

   Defilement is an unavoidable issue in the battle against rhino horn dealing. The contribution of degenerate authorities, both inside source nations and along dealing courses, permits criminal organizations to work without risk of punishment. Looking at the elements of debasement, understanding the inspirations of complicit people, and carrying out techniques to alleviate defilement are fundamental for powerful policing protection endeavors.

6. **Refinement in Carrying Strategies:**

   Criminal organizations utilize refined carrying strategies to dodge location and transport rhino horns across borders. From camouflage strategies to the utilization of fake shipments, these procedures challenge policing entrusted with catching unlawful natural life items. Examining the developing strategies utilized by dealers is urgent for adjusting and upgrading counter-carrying endeavors.

7. **Innovation and Dealing:**

   Headways in innovation have both worked with and provoked policing to battle rhino horn dealing. Criminal organizations influence encoded correspondence, dull web stages, and other mechanical devices to facilitate their exercises. Then again, progressives and specialists saddle innovation for following, observation, and insight gathering. The continuous innovative weapons contest among dealers and implementers shapes the scene of the illegal exchange.

8. **Worldwide Interest Driving Lawbreaker Interests:**

   The worldwide interest for rhino horns is a main thrust behind the contribution of criminal organizations. The financial impetuses provoked by this interest draw in coordinated wrongdoing, transforming rhino horn dealing into a rewarding endeavor. Looking at the elements of worldwide interest, figuring out buyer conduct, and tending to the underlying drivers of this request are essential parts of fighting criminal contribution in the exchange.

9. **Interconnections with Other Illegal Exchanges:**

   Rhino horn dealing is frequently interconnected with different types of illegal exchange, like medications, arms, and illegal exploitation. Criminal organizations differentiate their exercises to amplify benefits and limit gambles. Understanding these interconnections is fundamental for exhaustively tending to the more extensive difficulties presented by coordinated wrongdoing and upsetting the organizations associated with different unlawful exchanges.

10. **Courses and Travel Centers:**
Investigating the courses and travel center points utilized by criminal organizations gives significant experiences into the calculated parts of rhino horn dealing. Distinguishing key travel focuses and understanding the elements of transportation organizations can help experts in catching unlawful shipments and upsetting the progression of rhino horns from source to objective. Coordination between source, travel, and objective nations is basic for viable authorization.

11. **Aggressor Gatherings and Extremist Supporting:**
In specific districts, assailant gatherings and radicals have become engaged with rhino horn dealing for the purpose of supporting their exercises. The connection between natural life wrongdoing and rebellion represents extra difficulties for protection and security endeavors. Analyzing the nexus between aggressor gatherings and rhino horn dealing is fundamental for carrying out far reaching techniques that address both security and preservation concerns.

12. **Washing Through Legitimate Business sectors:**
Criminal organizations frequently exploit legitimate business sectors to wash rhino horns and legitimize their exchange. They might utilize lawful escape clauses, deceitful documentation, or shell organizations to move unlawful merchandise through genuine channels. Analyzing the weaknesses inside lawful business sectors and upgrading administrative structures is essential for shutting these roads and forestalling the washing of rhino horns.

13. **Shortcomings in Legitimate Systems:**
Shortcomings in legitimate systems, both locally and globally, add to the propagation of rhino horn dealing. Deficient punishments, indulgent authorization, and administrative holes set out open doors for criminal organizations to take advantage of provisos. Reinforcing legitimate structures, orchestrating guidelines across borders, and forcing extreme punishments for untamed life violations are fundamental parts of fighting these organizations.

14. **The Job of Agents and Intermediaries:**
Mediators and merchants assume a urgent part in working with rhino horn dealing. They go about as middle people among poachers and end buyers, planning the coordinated operations of the exchange. Understanding the jobs and inspirations of these people is urgent for disturbing the production network and destroying the crook networks included.

15. **Coordinated effort and Data Sharing:**
Powerful coordinated effort and data dividing among nations, policing, preservation associations, and INTERPOL are basic for fighting rhino horn dealing. Criminal organizations work across borders, requiring a planned and helpful

global reaction. Reinforcing joint effort components, sharing insight, and fitting requirement systems are basic for upsetting these organizations.

16. **Indictment and Lawful Activities:**
Indicting people engaged with rhino horn dealing is a critical part of destroying criminal organizations. Lawful activities should target poachers and dealers as well as those complicit in debasement and illegal tax avoidance. Reinforcing arraignment endeavors, improving worldwide legitimate participation, and guaranteeing that lawful results are comparable with the seriousness of the wrongdoings are fundamental for stopping criminal contribution in the exchange.

17. **Protection People group's Job in Knowledge:**
The protection local area assumes a vital part in get-together and sharing knowledge connected with rhino horn dealing. Preservation associations, specialists, and nearby networks frequently have significant data that can add to policing. Reinforcing organizations between the protection local area and policing upgrades the aggregate insight expected to battle criminal organizations.

18. **Public Mindfulness and Promotion:**
Public mindfulness and promotion endeavors are fundamental for preparing support against rhino horn dealing. By bringing issues to light about the outcomes of the unlawful exchange, scattering fantasies encompassing rhino horn use, and cultivating a feeling of obligation among shoppers, these drives add to decreasing the interest that supports criminal organizations.

19. **Tending to Financial Drivers:**
Tending to the financial drivers that drive people into the positions of poachers and dealers is basic for upsetting the enlistment pool for criminal organizations. Carrying out manageable elective livelihoods, advancing local area based protection drives, and tending to destitution related issues are necessary parts of an all encompassing way to deal with tending to the main drivers of rhino horn dealing.

20. **Connecting with Native People group:**

Drawing in native networks that possess rhino natural surroundings is fundamental for compelling protection and requirement endeavors. Perceiving the job of these networks as stewards of the land and including them in dynamic cycles upgrades protection results. Engaging native networks to oppose the impact of criminal organizations and encouraging a feeling of shared liability add to the drawn out maintainability of protection drives.

Chapter 3

Impact On Rhino Populations

The effect of poaching and unlawful exchange on rhino populaces involves grave worry, with broad ramifications for biodiversity, environments, and the worldwide protection exertion. This thorough paper tries to investigate the diverse effect of poaching on rhino populaces, including environmental repercussions, populace elements, and the more extensive ramifications for the endurance of these notorious species.

1. **Verifiable Setting of Rhino Populaces:**
   To comprehend the current effect on rhino populaces, it is urgent to dive into their verifiable setting. Rhinos, when broad across different mainlands, have confronted hundreds of years of abuse and territory misfortune. The authentic overhunting driven by interest for their horns, combined with pioneer time double-dealing, established the groundwork for the difficulties rhinos face today.

2. **Biological Job of Rhinos:**
   Rhinos assume a crucial part in forming their environments through different biological cycles. As uber herbivores, they add to seed dispersal, vegetation the executives, and living space change. Their taking care of propensities impact plant piece and conveyance, making a mosaic of scenes. Understanding the natural job of rhinos highlights their significance as cornerstone species and features the flowing impacts of populace decline.

3. **Populace Elements and Conceptive Difficulties:**
   The tireless poaching of rhinos has upset their normal populace elements, prompting slanted age designs and awkward nature in sex proportions. Poachers frequently target grown-up people, which has serious ramifications for reproducing populaces. Conceptive difficulties arise as a result, with expanded strain on excess people to keep up with reasonable reproducing populaces.

4. **Species-Explicit Effect: Dark Rhinos versus White Rhinos:**
   Different rhino species face unmistakable difficulties and show shifted reactions to poaching pressure. Dark rhinos, known for their lone and forceful way of

behaving, might be stronger to specific parts of poaching, however they are not safe to populace declines. White rhinos, showing a more friendly nature, face various difficulties, particularly concerning the disturbance of familial and social designs.

5. **Hereditary Variety and Inbreeding Dangers:**
As rhino populaces decline, the gamble of inbreeding increments, risking hereditary variety. Decreased hereditary variety reduces the versatile capability of populaces, making them more defenseless to illnesses and natural changes. Understanding the hereditary outcomes of poaching is crucial for long haul protection procedures pointed toward safeguarding the wellbeing and versatility of rhino populaces.

6. **Influence on Adolescents and Sub-Grown-ups:**
Poaching episodes excessively influence grown-up rhinos, yet the security influence on adolescents and sub-grown-ups is significant. The deficiency of grown-up people disturbs familial designs, influencing the direction and insurance that youthful rhinos get. The weakness of more youthful people to predation and ecological stressors increments, further compromising populace versatility.

7. **Segment Models and Populace Feasibility:**
Segment models give important devices to surveying the effect of poaching on the reasonability of rhino populaces. These models consider factors, for example, proliferation rates, death rates, and the age construction of populaces. Dissecting populace elements through segment demonstrating helps protectionists in anticipating future populace directions and conceiving designated mediations.

8. **Neighborhood Eliminations and Preservation Warnings:**
The tenacious poaching pressure has prompted nearby eliminations of rhino populaces in unambiguous districts. Once-flourishing populaces have dwindled to impractical levels, sounding preservation warnings. The deficiency of rhino populaces decreases biodiversity as well as disturbs biological cycles that depend on the presence of these notable megafauna.

9. **Influence on Biological systems and Biodiversity:**
Rhinos are fundamental to the working of their environments, and their decay resounds across the whole natural web. From affecting vegetation design to supporting other natural life species through their biological jobs, rhinos add to the general wellbeing and biodiversity of their territories. The effect on environments stretches out past the departure of a solitary animal categories, influencing interconnected connections and natural adjusts.

10. **Trophic Fountains and Herbivore Elements:**
The decay of rhino populaces starts trophic fountains, changing herbivore elements inside biological systems. With less super herbivores impacting vegetation, plant networks might encounter shifts in sythesis and thickness.
These progressions overflow through the food web, influencing herbivore-

subordinate hunters and making a far reaching influence all through the biological system.

11. **Intrusive Species and Territory Changes:**
The shortfall of rhinos because of poaching takes into consideration uncontrolled development of specific plant species, possibly prompting environment changes. Obtrusive plants might multiply without any rhino brushing, modifying the design of biological systems. Understanding the environmental outcomes of rhino populace decline illuminates protection systems pointed toward moderating the effect on territories.

12. **Prairie Biological systems and Fire Elements:**
Rhinos, especially white rhinos, are fundamental to field environments' fire elements. Their particular eating keeps up with open meadows, diminishing fuel burden and restricting the spread of out of control fires. The downfall of rhino populaces disturbs this regular cycle, possibly prompting adjusted fire systems with suggestions for vegetation construction and biodiversity.

13. **Preservation Holds and Safeguarded Regions:**
Preservation holds and safeguarded regions are basic for saving rhino populaces, giving a safe-haven where they can flourish. Be that as it may, these regions face expanding dangers from poaching, requiring improved security measures. Surveying the effect of poaching on safeguarded regions illuminates versatile administration systems to invigorate these fundamental spaces for rhino protection.

14. **Monetary Effect on The travel industry:**
Rhinos contribute fundamentally to the travel industry income in numerous districts, drawing in untamed life devotees from around the world. The monetary effect of poaching stretches out past direct protection costs, enveloping misfortunes in the travel industry income, occupations, and related ventures. Understanding the financial repercussions features the interconnectedness of protection and nearby economies.

15. **Local area Relations and Livelihoods:**
Networks living close to rhino environments frequently endure the worst part of the effect of poaching. The deficiency of the travel industry income, natural debasement, and expected clashes among networks and protection endeavors highlight the mind boggling social elements of rhino preservation. Fortifying people group relations and tending to financial difficulties are vital parts of compelling preservation procedures.

16. **Worldwide Protection Drives and Coordinated efforts:**
The effect of poaching on rhino populaces requires worldwide protection drives and coordinated efforts. Worldwide endeavors, like those drove by preservation associations, legislatures, and non-administrative substances, assume a significant part in tending to the complex difficulties looked by rhinos. Cooperative

systems incorporate enemy of poaching measures, territory assurance, local area commitment, and promotion.

17. **Job of Innovation in Preservation:**
Mechanical headways offer imaginative answers for checking and safeguarding rhino populaces. From robots and satellite symbolism to sensor innovations and GPS beacons, these instruments upgrade preservationists' capacity to recognize poaching episodes, track rhino developments, and accumulate significant information for informed navigation.

18. **Movement and Populace Expansion:**
Movement and populace expansion drives expect to support rhino populaces and increment hereditary variety. These intercessions include moving rhinos from regions with stable populaces to those confronting decline. The achievement and difficulties of movement systems contribute significant experiences to traditionalists pursuing practical populace the board.

19. **Strategy and Lawful Systems:**
Viable arrangement and legitimate systems are urgent for combatting poaching and safeguarding rhino populaces. Regulation tending to natural life wrongdoing, punishments for poaching and dealing, and global participation through arrangements, for example, Refers to shape the establishment for protection endeavors. Assessing the viability of existing strategies and upholding for more grounded lawful structures are continuous goals.

20. **Public Mindfulness and Training:**

Public mindfulness and training efforts are indispensable parts of preservation endeavors to alleviate the effect of poaching on rhino populaces. By cultivating a comprehension of the natural significance of rhinos, dispersing fantasies encompassing their horns, and drawing in networks in protection drives, these missions add to a more extensive cultural obligation to saving these grand species.

3.1 Statistics on rhino population decline

The downfall of rhino populaces is a basic protection issue that requests consideration and activity. This thorough exposition plans to dig into the insights encompassing the decay of rhino populaces, investigating the numbers, patterns, and hidden factors adding to the dubious condition of these notorious species. Through an exhaustive investigation of the accessible information, we mean to give a complete comprehension of the extent of the emergency and the earnestness of protection endeavors.

1. **Verifiable Rhino Populace Numbers:**
Understanding the verifiable setting is fundamental for getting a handle on the seriousness of the ongoing rhino populace decline. At the turn of the twentieth 100 years, different rhino species, including the white rhinoceros (Ceratotherium simum) and the dark rhinoceros (Diceros bicornis), meandered

assorted territories across Africa and Asia. Authentic appraisals recommend altogether larger numbers than the current populaces, showing the greatness of the decay.

2. **White Rhinoceros (Ceratotherium simum) Populace Patterns:**
The white rhinoceros, local to Southern Africa, has encountered critical populace vacillations throughout the long term. Verifiable highs in the mid twentieth century were trailed by an uncommon downfall because of broad poaching and territory misfortune. Preservation endeavors, especially in South Africa, prompted a wonderful recuperation in the last option part of the hundred years. Be that as it may, late years have seen a resurgence in poaching episodes, taking steps to switch the positive patterns.

3. **Dark Rhinoceros (Diceros bicornis) Populace Patterns:**
The dark rhinoceros, appropriated across different African living spaces, confronted serious populace declines during the last 50% of the twentieth hundred years. Escalated poaching driven by interest for their horns prompted a stunning decrease in numbers. Preservation drives, like movement and environment security, have added to populace recuperations in specific regions. Regardless, steady dangers, especially from poaching, keep on testing the dark rhino's preservation status.

4. **Asian Rhinoceros Species: Javan and Sumatran Rhinos:**
The Javan rhinoceros (Rhinoceros sondaicus) and Sumatran rhinoceros (Dicerorhinus sumatrensis) are basically jeopardized species local to Asia. The two species have encountered extreme populace declines, essentially because of environment misfortune and poaching. The Javan rhino is currently restricted to a solitary populace in Ujung Kulon Public Park, Indonesia, while the Sumatran rhino faces significantly more shaky conditions, with divided populaces in Sumatra and Borneo.

5. **Worldwide Rhinoceros Populace Appraisals:**
Ongoing worldwide evaluations show a complete rhinoceros populace of roughly 27,000 people across all species. This number mirrors a critical decay from verifiable highs and highlights the continuous dangers looked by rhino populaces around the world. The dispersion of these people differs among species, with the greater part amassed in unambiguous locales, featuring the lopsided effect of poaching and natural surroundings misfortune.

6. **Poaching Occurrences and Unlawful Exchange:**
Poaching stays the essential danger to rhino populaces, driven by the interest for their horns in unlawful business sectors. Measurable information on poaching episodes uncover disturbing patterns, with a flood in criminal operations lately. In spite of protection endeavors and hostile to poaching measures, criminal organizations keep on taking advantage of weaknesses, prompting a steady cost for rhino populaces.

7. **Rhino Horn Seizures and Dealing Patterns:**
   Following the unlawful exchange rhino horns gives experiences into the scale and elements of dealing organizations. Seizure information at boundaries, air terminals, and different places of travel uncover the degree of the worldwide market for rhino horns. The geological conveyance of seizures and dealing courses offers significant data for policing preservation associations attempting to destroy these lawbreaker organizations.

8. **Provincial Differences in Poaching Rates:**
   Rhino poaching rates fluctuate essentially across districts, mirroring the different difficulties looked by preservationists. Southern Africa, home to most of the world's white rhinos, has been a focal point for poaching episodes. Conversely, certain populaces in Asia face extraordinary dangers, including environment fracture and human-natural life struggle. Breaking down local inconsistencies helps tailor protection techniques to address explicit difficulties.

9. **Protection Examples of overcoming adversity:**
   In the midst of the terrible measurements, there are examples of fruitful rhino preservation. A populaces have bounced back because of committed preservation endeavors, including natural surroundings security, hostile to poaching measures, and local area commitment. Examples of overcoming adversity feature the viability of key intercessions and the significance of supported obligation to rhino preservation.

10. **Effect of Coronavirus on Poaching:**
    The Coronavirus pandemic acquainted extra difficulties with rhino preservation, influencing both subsidizing and on-the-ground endeavors. The financial repercussions of the pandemic, combined with disturbances in movement and the travel industry, made conditions that poachers took advantage of. Understanding the pandemic's effect on rhino populaces gives bits of knowledge into the strength of protection endeavors during worldwide emergencies.

11. **Monetary Valuation of Rhino Protection:**
    The monetary worth of rhino protection reaches out past the natural worth of safeguarding biodiversity. Rhinos contribute fundamentally to the travel industry income, giving position and supporting neighborhood economies. Monetary valuation concentrates on offer experiences into the monetary advantages of monitoring rhino populaces, presenting a convincing defense for proceeded with interest in their security.

12. **Preservation Subsidizing and Backing:**
    Dissecting the monetary help coordinated towards rhino preservation uncovers the size of interest in enemy of poaching measures, environment security, and local area commitment. Understanding subsidizing patterns surveys the ampleness of assets dispensed to battle the complex difficulties confronting rhino populaces and distinguishes regions where extra help is pivotal.

13. **Joint effort Among Partners:**

    The battle against rhino populace decline includes a horde of partners, including states, non-legislative associations, neighborhood networks, and the worldwide public. Dissecting cooperative endeavors reveals insight into the viability of organizations in executing extensive preservation methodologies. Effective joint efforts frequently rise above lines and areas, mirroring the interconnected idea of rhino protection.

14. **Lawful Systems and Administrative Measures:**

    Lawful systems and administrative measures assume a crucial part in molding the scene of rhino preservation. Investigating the adequacy of existing regulations, punishments for natural life violations, and peaceful accords, for example, Refers to gives experiences into the difficulties looked by specialists. Reinforcing lawful structures is critical for discouraging poaching and upsetting unlawful exchange organizations.

15. **Job of Innovation in Observing and Implementation:**

    Innovative headways have altered the field of rhino protection. From the utilization of robots for airborne reconnaissance to GPS beacons for checking individual rhinos, innovation upgrades the proficiency of hostile to poaching endeavors.

    Surveying the combination of innovation into protection procedures gives a brief look into the developing instruments used to shield rhino populaces.

16. **Public Mindfulness and Backing:**

    Public mindfulness and backing efforts assume an imperative part in preparing support for rhino preservation. Examining the effect of these missions gives bits of knowledge into their viability in scattering fantasies encompassing rhino horns, encouraging a feeling of obligation among purchasers, and producing public strain for more grounded protection measures.

17. **Difficulties and Future Viewpoint:**

In spite of preservation endeavors, rhino populaces keep on confronting considerable difficulties. Looking at these difficulties, including continuous poaching dangers, living space misfortune, and worldwide market elements, advises the plan regarding future protection methodologies. The future standpoint for rhino populaces relies upon versatile methodologies, supported cooperation, and an aggregate obligation to their protection.

3.2 Ecological consequences of rhino poaching

The natural outcomes of rhino poaching stretch out a long ways past the prompt loss of individual creatures. Rhino species, including the white rhinoceros (Ceratotherium simum) and the dark rhinoceros (Diceros bicornis), are fundamental parts of their environments, assuming basic parts in forming biodiversity, keeping up with territory structure, and affecting natural cycles. This complete article investigates the multi-layered natural outcomes of rhino poaching, analyzing influences on vegetation, trophic elements, biological system versatility, and the more extensive ramifications for biodiversity preservation.

1. **Rhino as a Cornerstone Animal types:**
   Rhinos are viewed as cornerstone species in their environments, meaning their presence to a great extent affects the construction and capability of their natural surroundings. As super herbivores, rhinos apply impact through their taking care of propensities, molding vegetation, and in a roundabout way influencing various different species. The expulsion of rhinos through poaching disturbs these biological cycles, setting off a fountain of results.

2. **Impact on Vegetation Construction:**
   Rhinos are vital for keeping up with open meadows and forestalling woody infringement through their specific nibbling. White rhinos, specifically, assume a vital part in molding the design of meadow environments.
   The decrease in rhino populaces because of poaching brings about uncontrolled vegetation development, adjusting the creation and thickness of plant networks.

3. **Seed Dispersal and Plant Enlistment:**
   Rhinos contribute altogether to seed dispersal, helping with the enlistment of different plant species. Their stomach related frameworks are adjusted to handling seeds, and the scattered seeds frequently benefit from the supplement rich dung, giving an optimal climate to germination. The downfall of rhino populaces upsets this seed dispersal component, influencing the elements of plant networks.

4. **Living space Change and Biodiversity:**
   Rhinos alter their territories through their taking care of and floundering ways of behaving. These changes make a mosaic of microhabitats, helping a different cluster of animal groups. The deficiency of rhinos disturbs these living space changes, possibly prompting homogenization and decreased biodiversity. The perplexing connections among rhinos and different species feature the inter-connectedness of biological systems.

5. **Trophic Fountains and Herbivore Elements:**
   Rhinos are central members in trophic fountains, affecting the overflow and conduct of different herbivores. Their particular munching keeps a harmony among grasses and woody plants, forming the vegetation structure. The down-fall of rhinos can set off trophic fountains, influencing herbivore elements and, accordingly, hunters and scroungers reliant upon herbivore populaces.

6. **Influence on Meadow Environments:**
   The decay of rhino populaces significantly affects meadow biological systems. Without rhinos, there is a gamble of unrestrained grass development, prompting modified fire systems, diminished plant variety, and changes in supplement

cycling. Understanding the environmental outcomes of rhino poaching on fields is vital for creating preservation methodologies that address these difficulties.

7. **Fire Elements and Vegetation Arrangement:**
Rhinos, especially white rhinos, impact fire elements in meadow environments. Their specific brushing decreases fuel load, restricting the spread of fierce blazes. The decay of rhinos can bring about expanded fuel load, modifying fire systems and possibly prompting changes in vegetation organization. Investigating the interchange between rhinos, fire, and vegetation gives experiences into biological system versatility.

8. **Influence on Jeopardized Plant Species:**
Rhinos add to the preservation of different plant species, including those recorded as jeopardized. Through seed dispersal and environment changes, rhinos assume a part in keeping up with the populaces of plants that may somehow confront dangers. The decrease in rhino populaces endangers the protection status of these plant species, further featuring the interconnected idea of biodiversity.

9. **Changed Soil Supplement Cycling:**
Rhinos impact soil supplement pushing through their taking care of and floundering exercises. Their manure gives a supplement rich substrate to vegetation development, upgrading the general fruitfulness of the dirt. The decay of rhinos can upset this supplement cycling, possibly prompting changes in soil piece and influencing the efficiency of plant networks.

10. **Natural Jobs of Various Rhino Species:**
Different rhino species display one of a kind environmental jobs in view of their ways of behaving and natural surroundings. White rhinos, with their munching propensities, impact meadow biological systems, while dark rhinos, known for their perusing inclinations, assume a part in molding woody vegetation. Understanding the natural subtleties of every species is fundamental for designated protection endeavors.

11. **Influence on Invertebrate People group:**
Rhinos impact vertebrate networks as well as invertebrate networks in their biological systems. Their exercises, for example, floundering and taking care of, make microhabitats that help a different exhibit of spineless creatures. The decay of rhinos can prompt changes in the overflow and variety of spineless creatures, with possible implications for biological system processes.

12. **Interruption of Harmonious Connections:**
Rhinos partake in harmonious associations with different species, remembering birds that feed for ectoparasites drawn to rhino skin. The deficiency of rhinos upsets these harmonious connections, influencing the organic entities that rely upon rhinos for food or living space. Analyzing these complicated connections gives experiences into the more extensive biological results of rhino poaching.

13. **Human-Untamed life Struggle and Biological system Wellbeing:**
    The downfall of rhino populaces can fuel human-untamed life clashes as herbivores, looking for elective food sources, infringe on rural terrains. Relieving such contentions is fundamental for cultivating concurrence among people and natural life.
    The soundness of biological systems is unpredictably connected to the equilibrium of herbivore populaces, accentuating the significance of rhinos in keeping up with environment strength.

14. **Versatility of Biological systems to Aggravations:**
    Rhinos add to the strength of environments, upgrading their capacity to endure and recuperate from unsettling influences like dry seasons or rapidly spreading fires. The deficiency of rhinos might think twice about versatility, making biological systems more powerless against outer tensions. Understanding the job of rhinos in environment strength illuminates preservation methodologies pointed toward keeping up with the soundness of regular frameworks.

15. **Territory Fracture and Network:**
    Rhino poaching can add to territory fracture, disengaging populaces and restricting hereditary trade between people. Keeping up with living space network is pivotal for the drawn out feasibility of rhino populaces. Evaluating the environmental outcomes of living space discontinuity gives experiences into the difficulties looked by rhinos in divided scenes.

16. **Trophic Minimizing and Environment Awkward nature:**
    The downfall of megaherbivores like rhinos can prompt trophic downsizing, a peculiarity where the deficiency of top hunters or herbivores overflows through the food web, influencing lower trophic levels. Environment uneven characters might happen subsequently, with possible ramifications for vegetation, herbivores, and hunters. Understanding trophic elements is fundamental for anticipating and relieving these uneven characters.

17. **Environment Administrations Given by Rhinos:**
    Rhinos add to different environment administrations, including seed dispersal, living space adjustment, and support of biodiversity. The downfall of rhinos can think twice about administrations, influencing the general wellbeing and usefulness of environments. Assessing the environment administrations given by rhinos highlights their significance for human prosperity and natural supportability.

18. **Protection Procedures and Environmental Reclamation:**
    Creating viable protection methodologies requires a comprehensive comprehension of the environmental outcomes of rhino poaching. Preservation drives shouldn't just zero in on safeguarding rhinos yet in addition address more extensive environment elements.
    Natural rebuilding endeavors, including environment restoration and renewed

introduction programs, assume a urgent part in relieving the effects of rhino poaching on biological systems.

19. **Worldwide Ramifications for Biodiversity Protection:**

The biological results of rhino poaching stretch out past individual species or environments. Rhinos, as cornerstone species, impact the wellbeing of whole scenes and add to worldwide biodiversity. The deficiency of rhinos has suggestions for the equilibrium of environments around the world, stressing the interconnected idea of preservation endeavors on a worldwide scale.

3.3 Efforts and challenges in rhino conservation

Rhino preservation remains at a basic point, with coordinated endeavors in progress to address the difficulties undermining the endurance of these notorious species. This exposition dives into the multi-layered scene of rhino protection, investigating the continuous drives, imaginative techniques, and determined difficulties looked by moderates around the world. From hostile to poaching measures and living space insurance to local area commitment and global cooperation, the aggregate work to get the fate of rhinos requires a nuanced comprehension of the intricacies in question.

1. **Against Poaching Drives:**
1. **Expanding Watches and Observation:**
   One of the essential difficulties in rhino preservation is the steady danger of poaching for their horns. Hostile to poaching drives include expanding watches and utilizing progressed observation advances in rhino territories. Park officers and policing work energetically to screen and protect these regions, utilizing drones, camera traps, and different apparatuses to identify and deflect poaching exercises.

2. **Preparing and Preparing Against Poaching Groups:**
   Putting resources into the preparation and preparing of against poaching groups is pivotal for upgrading their viability in the field. Particular preparation programs center around following, natural life policing, compromise. Furnishing these groups with the fundamental hardware, for example, night-vision goggles and specialized gadgets, reinforces their capacity to answer poaching occurrences quickly and conclusively.

3. **Joint effort with Nearby People group:**

Connecting with neighborhood networks in enemy of poaching endeavors is fundamental for making an organization of help. Local area individuals, who frequently possess or live close to rhino natural surroundings, can act as extra eyes and ears on the ground.

Cooperative drives incorporate local area based enemy of poaching watches, bringing issues to light, and cultivating a feeling of shared liability regarding rhino preservation.

II. Natural surroundings Security and The board:

1. **Development and Network of Safeguarded Regions:**
   Saving rhino environments requires the security of existing regions as well as the extension and network of safeguarded zones. Protection associations work to get extra land for rhino populaces, making passages that consider hereditary trade and keep up with natural network. This approach mitigates the dangers related with territory discontinuity.

2. **Territory Recovery and Rebuilding:**
   In regions where rhino territories have been corrupted, territory recovery and rebuilding endeavors are vital. These drives include establishing local vegetation, controlling obtrusive species, and reestablishing water sources. Restoring de-based natural surroundings improves the conveying limit of the land, offering feasible help for rhino populaces.

3. **Movement and Populace Increase:**

Movement includes moving rhinos from regions with stable populaces to those confronting decline. This procedure means to lay out or reinforce populaces in appropriate natural surroundings, expanding hereditary variety and relieving the gamble of inbreeding. Fruitful movement programs require fastidious preparation, checking, and versatile administration.

III. Innovation Reconciliation in Preservation:

1. **Robots and Elevated Observation:**
   The coordination of innovation, like robots, has altered rhino protection endeavors. Drones give airborne reconnaissance, taking into consideration continuous checking of rhino environments and early location of poaching exercises. The utilization of warm imaging and GPS innovation upgrades the viability of robot based observation in testing territories.

2. **Sensor Advancements and GPS beacons:**
   Conveying sensor advances and GPS beacons on rhinos gives significant information to analysts and preservationists. These gadgets screen rhino developments, assemble data on conduct, and proposition experiences into environment use. The information created adds to logical comprehension and helps in the definition of designated preservation procedures.

3. **DNA Examination and Hereditary Observing:**

DNA examination is utilized for hereditary observing of rhino populaces. This approach surveys hereditary variety, distinguish people, and track genealogies. Hereditary checking is fundamental for understanding the wellbeing of populaces, distinguishing potential inbreeding dangers, and illuminating rearing projects pointed toward protecting hereditary variety.

IV. Local area Commitment and Feasible Turn of events:

1. **Schooling and Mindfulness Projects:**
   Local area commitment is crucial for the progress of rhino preservation endeavors. Training and mindfulness programs target neighborhood networks, schools, and organizations, cultivating a comprehension of the natural significance of rhinos. Dispersing legends connected with rhino horns and featuring their part in environments add to a culture of protection.

2. **Occupation Backing and Manageable Turn of events:**
   Tending to the financial requirements of networks living close to rhino natural surroundings is fundamental for encouraging positive associations with preservation endeavors. Occupation support programs, for example, elective pay age and feasible advancement drives, expect to diminish reliance on regular assets and mitigate destitution, at last decreasing the tension on rhino environments.

3. **Local area Based Preservation Drives:**

Engaging neighborhood networks to effectively take part in rhino protection is accomplished through local area based drives. These may incorporate the foundation of local area conservancies, where networks have a stake in the administration and advantages got from rhino populaces. Cooperative administration models advance concurrence among natural life and individuals.

V. Global Coordinated effort and Promotion:

1. **Cross-Boundary Joint effort:**
   Rhino preservation frequently rises above public lines, requiring cooperative endeavors among nations. Cross-line cooperation includes sharing knowledge, blending protection methodologies, and tending to transboundary issues, for example, dealing courses. Territorial drives fortify the aggregate reaction to the difficulties looked by rhino populaces.

2. **Worldwide Preservation Associations:**
   Worldwide preservation associations assume a critical part in supporting rhino protection endeavors. These associations give financing, specialized mastery, and promotion on a worldwide scale. Cooperative tasks including various partners add to the execution of thorough protection techniques.

3. **Backing for Strategy Change:**

Promotion endeavors center around impacting strategy change at public and global levels. Advocates work to reinforce untamed life assurance regulations, increment punishments for poaching and dealing, and advance the consideration of rhino protection in more extensive ecological plans. Affecting approach is key to establishing a climate helpful for compelling protection.

VI. Challenges in Rhino Preservation:

1. **Poaching and Unlawful Natural life Exchange:**
   The industrious test of poaching and the unlawful natural life exchange stays an impressive danger to rhino populaces. Regardless of escalated enemy of poaching endeavors, criminal organizations keep on taking advantage of weaknesses, driven by the rewarding interest for rhino horns in unlawful business sectors.

2. **Territory Misfortune and Fracture:**
   Territory misfortune and fracture result from human infringement, agribusiness, and foundation improvement. These elements diminish the accessible space for rhino populaces, prompting confined territories that posture dangers to hereditary variety and by and large populace wellbeing.

3. **Human-Natural life Struggle:**
   As rhino living spaces shrivel, clashes among rhinos and nearby networks might heighten. Crop strikes by herbivores looking for elective food sources can prompt retaliatory killings, further stressing the fragile harmony between human necessities and natural life preservation.

4. **Insufficient Financing and Assets:**
   Rhino protection endeavors frequently face difficulties connected with insufficient financing and assets. The monetary weight of hostile to poaching measures, living space security, and local area commitment requires supported speculation. Contending needs for preservation assets can block the exhaustive execution of protection techniques.

5. **Political Unsteadiness and Debasement:**
   Areas with rhino populaces might confront political unsteadiness and defilement, which can subvert successful preservation endeavors. Powerless administration, absence of policing, defilement inside organizations entrusted with safeguarding natural life make ideal circumstances for poaching and unlawful exchange.

6. **Zoonotic Sickness Dangers:**
   The rise of zoonotic illnesses represents an expected danger to rhino populaces. Sickness transmission among people and rhinos can prompt wellbeing emergencies inside populaces. Overseeing and moderating infection gambles require thorough checking and biosecurity measures.

7. **Environmental Change and Living space Movements:**

Environmental change represents a danger to rhino territories, prompting shifts in vegetation designs, modified water accessibility, and changes in temperature. Adjusting to these progressions requires dynamic protection methodologies that record for the effects of environmental change on rhino populaces and their biological systems.

Chapter 4

Human Cost Of Trafficking

Illegal exploitation, a grave infringement of common liberties, is a worldwide peculiarity that incurs vast languishing over people, families, and networks. This far reaching exposition investigates the complex human expense of dealing, revealing insight into the physical, mental, and financial outcomes looked by casualties. From the strategies utilized by dealers to the difficulties survivors experience during and after their difficulty, understanding the human expense is pivotal for molding powerful enemy of dealing procedures and it is killed to cultivate a reality where double-dealing.

1. **Figuring out Illegal exploitation:**
1. **Definition and Types of Dealing:**
   Illegal exploitation is regularly characterized as the enrollment, transportation, move, holding onto, or receipt of people through power, misrepresentation, or pressure with the end goal of abuse. This abuse takes different structures, including constrained work, sex dealing, kid double-dealing, and organ dealing. Looking at the assorted indications of dealing is fundamental for getting a handle on the broadness of its effect on people.
2. **Dealing Strategies and Enrollment Techniques:**

Dealers utilize complex strategies to bait, control, and control their casualties. Enrollment strategies range from misleading commitments of business and training to kidnapping and intimidation. Understanding the techniques dealers use gives bits of knowledge into the weaknesses they exploit, enabling enemy of dealing endeavors to target underlying drivers.

II. Actual Results of Dealing:

1. **Constrained Work and Shady Working Circumstances:**
   Casualties of constrained work persevere through tiring working circumstances in different enterprises, from farming and development to homegrown work

and assembling. Shady practices incorporate extended periods of time, deficient wages, absence of security measures, and actual maltreatment. Analyzing the actual cost for dealt people features the earnestness of tending to work abuse.

2. **Sexual Abuse and Wellbeing Dangers:**
Sex dealing subjects casualties to serious physical and sexual maltreatment. The consistent danger of viciousness, openness to physically communicated contaminations (STIs), and the shortfall of medical care add to a horde of wellbeing gambles. Examining the actual results of sexual double-dealing highlights the earnest requirement for complete help for survivors.

3. **Human Pirating and Perilous Excursions:**

Transients looking for a superior life might succumb to human pirating, frequently covering with dealing. The dangerous excursions coordinated by bootleggers open people to actual risks, including savagery, starvation, and cruel natural circumstances. Dissecting the actual cost of these excursions underlines the requirement for defensive measures for weak transients.

III. Mental Effect on Dealing Survivors:

1. **Injury and Post-Awful Pressure Issue (PTSD):**
Dealing survivors as often as possible experience extreme mental injury coming about because of the maltreatment, compulsion, and double-dealing they persevere. Post-horrible pressure problem (PTSD) is a typical result, appearing as meddlesome recollections, bad dreams, and profound pain. Understanding the mental effect illuminates injury informed ways to deal with help survivors on their way to recuperation.

2. **capture-bonding and Mental Control:**
Mental control by dealers frequently prompts capture-bonding, where casualties foster a bond with their detainers as an endurance component. Examining the mental elements included reveals insight into the intricacy of casualty culprit connections and illuminates mediations that address the mental obstructions survivors face.

3. **Derision and Social Reintegration:**

Dealing survivors frequently experience cultural disgrace and separation upon reintegration. Inspecting the mental effect of social dismissal features the significance of local area mindfulness and backing projects to neutralize shame and encourage a climate helpful for survivors' recuperating.

IV. Financial Ramifications for Dealing Casualties:

1. **Monetary Double-dealing and Obligation Servitude:**
Many dealing casualties face monetary double-dealing, frequently caught under

water servitude. Examining the financial results of obligation servitude highlights the requirement for mediations that address the main drivers of weakness, including neediness and absence of monetary open doors.

2. **Loss of Training and Expertise Improvement:**
   Dealt kids frequently lose admittance to training, blocking their long haul financial possibilities. Inspecting the effect of disturbed schooling highlights the significance of instructive intercessions for dealt youngsters, furnishing them with the abilities vital for a more promising time to come.

3. **Legitimate Outcomes and Admittance to Equity:**

Survivors of dealing might experience legitimate results, including detainment and removal, further compounding their weakness. Examining the financial effect of legitimate difficulties features the requirement for extensive lawful help to guarantee admittance to equity for survivors.

V. Weak Populaces and Dealing Elements:

1. **Orientation Based Brutality and Double-dealing:**
   Ladies and young ladies are excessively impacted by dealing, encountering orientation based brutality and abuse. Breaking down the interconnection of dealing with orientation elements uncovers the particular difficulties looked by female casualties and illuminates orientation delicate intercessions.

2. **Kid Dealing and Double-dealing:**
   Kids are especially helpless against dealing, confronting abuse in different structures, including constrained work, youngster soldiering, and sexual double-dealing. Inspecting the particular elements of kid dealing accentuates the requirement for youngster driven ways to deal with anticipation, assurance, and recovery.

3. **Movement and Dealing Interconnections:**

The crossing point of movement and dealing is a perplexing peculiarity, with transients frequently succumbing to dealing during their excursion or in the objective country. Examining the interconnections among movement and dealing illuminates designated intercessions that address the weaknesses looked by transients.

VI. Challenges in Recognizing and Helping Dealing Casualties:

1. **Underreporting and Secret Nature of Dealing:**
   Illegal exploitation remains generally concealed due to underreporting, apprehension about backlashes, and the covert idea of the wrongdoing. Breaking down the difficulties in distinguishing dealing casualties features the requirement for mindfulness crusades, preparing for cutting edge responders, and measures to construct trust inside weak networks.

2. **Absence of Coordination and Data Sharing:**
Viable enemy of dealing endeavors require coordination and data dividing between policing, administrative associations (NGOs), and worldwide organizations. Analyzing the difficulties in cooperation highlights the significance of multi-organization draws near and the sharing of best practices to upgrade the recognizable proof and help of dealing casualties.

3. **Weaknesses in Casualty Security and Backing:**

Casualty assurance and backing projects might confront deficiencies in giving exhaustive consideration, including haven, medical services, and lawful help. Investigating these difficulties educates the improvement regarding casualty focused administrations and the advancement of reasonable emotionally supportive networks for survivors.

VII. The Job of Innovation in Combatting Dealing:

1. **Online Abuse and Cybercrime:**
Headways in innovation have worked with new types of dealing, including on the web abuse and cybercrime. Researching the job of innovation in dealing elements features the requirement for creative systems, worldwide collaboration, and lawful structures to address arising difficulties.

2. **Utilization of Innovation for Avoidance and Mindfulness:**
Innovation assumes a vital part in forestalling dealing through mindfulness crusades, schooling programs, and the spread of data. Analyzing effective purposes of innovation in counteraction highlights the potential for utilizing advanced devices to enable networks and people against dealing.

3. **Information and Investigation for Against Dealing Endeavors:**

Information investigation and man-made consciousness can possibly upgrade hostile to dealing endeavors by recognizing examples, patterns, and potential dealing organizations. Dissecting the job of information in combatting dealing educates the advancement regarding information driven techniques and mediations.

VIII. Lawful Systems and Global Participation:

1. **Worldwide Shows and Settlements:**
The battle against dealing is upheld by worldwide shows and settlements, for example, the Assembled Countries Convention to Forestall, Smother and Rebuff Dealing with People. Looking at the lawful structures features the significance of worldwide participation and the requirement for steady implementation to battle dealing.

2. **Challenges in Arraignment and Responsibility:**
Arraigning dealers and considering them responsible for their violations presents

difficulties, including jurisdictional issues and the hesitance of casualties to affirm. Examining the obstacles in arraignment stresses the requirement for lawful changes, casualty assurance measures, and global coordinated effort to guarantee equity for survivors.

3. **Common freedoms Based Ways to deal with Hostile to Dealing:**

Taking on common liberties based approaches is key to viable enemy of dealing endeavors. Looking at the job of common freedoms structures illuminates intercessions that focus on the nobility, organization, and prosperity of dealing survivors, advancing an all encompassing and casualty focused approach.

IX. Restoration and Reintegration of Dealing Survivors:

1. **All encompassing Help Administrations for Survivors:**
Recovery and reintegration of dealing survivors need all encompassing help administrations, including psychological well-being guiding, professional preparation, and instructive open doors. Examining fruitful recovery models advises the improvement regarding thorough projects that address the assorted necessities of survivors.

2. **Local area Based Ways to deal with Reintegration:**
Local area based reintegration approaches include enabling nearby networks to help the recuperation of dealing survivors. Looking at fruitful local area based models highlights the significance of encouraging a comprehensive and strong climate for survivors to revamp their lives.

3. **Long haul Effect and Examples of overcoming adversity:**

Surveying the drawn out effect of recovery and reintegration endeavors gives experiences into the examples of overcoming adversity of survivors who have defeated the difficulties of dealing. Looking at positive results illuminates future mediations and accentuates the strength and organization of survivors.

X. Avoidance Systems and Instruction:

1. **Preventive Instruction and Mindfulness:**
Preventive training and mindfulness crusades assume a vital part in outfitting networks with the information and abilities to perceive and forestall dealing. Dissecting fruitful instructive drives advises the improvement regarding viable counteraction procedures that target weak populaces.

2. **Engaging Weak People group:**
Enabling weak networks includes tending to underlying drivers, like destitution, absence of training, and orientation disparity. Inspecting effective strengthening programs highlights the significance of local area driven drives that form versatility and diminish the weakness of people to dealing.

3. Official Measures and Strategy Support:

Regulative measures and strategy backing add to the counteraction of dealing by making legitimate structures, upholding punishments, and pushing for foundational changes. Investigating the effect of administrative endeavors educates the advancement regarding proof based approaches that improve anticipation systems.

4.1 Involvement of local communities in poaching

The contribution of neighborhood networks in poaching is a diverse issue that requires a nuanced comprehension of the financial, social, and natural variables impacting people to participate in unlawful untamed life exercises. This article digs into the complicated elements encompassing the support of neighborhood networks in poaching, analyzing the underlying drivers, influence on preservation endeavors, and techniques for encouraging local area commitment in natural life assurance.

1. **Financial Elements:**
1. **Neediness and Vocation Tensions:**
   One of the essential drivers behind the contribution of nearby networks in poaching is neediness and financial difficulty. In locales where elective business valuable open doors are restricted, people might go to poaching for of creating pay to help themselves and their families. Looking at the financial inspirations driving poaching highlights the significance of tending to neediness as a principal part of natural life preservation systems.
2. **Absence of Work Open doors:**
   In regions with high joblessness rates, people might consider poaching to be a suitable choice for financial endurance. The shortfall of formal business valuable open doors, combined with restricted admittance to schooling and expertise improvement, adds to a pattern of reliance on normal assets for food. Examining the connection between work open doors and poaching features the requirement for thorough financial advancement drives.
3. **Monetary Inconsistencies and Disparity:**

Monetary inconsistencies inside nearby networks can make a feeling of imbalance, driving a few people to see poaching as a method for tending to apparent treacheries. Inspecting the effect of monetary imbalances on poaching association highlights the significance of advancing comprehensive turn of events and fair dissemination of assets.

II. Social and Customary Practices:

1. **Conventional Convictions and Customs:**
   In specific networks, conventional convictions and customs might add to the interest for untamed life items, cultivating a social acknowledgment of

poaching. Creatures and their body parts might be utilized in customs, conventional medication, or as superficial points of interest, sustaining the pattern of unlawful natural life exchange. Understanding the social elements of poaching is fundamental for executing socially touchy protection systems.

2. **Prize Hunting and Social Importance:**
Prize hunting, while disputable, is viewed as a socially critical practice in certain districts. The longing for esteem and social acknowledgment drives people to partake in hunting exercises, including those that might be unreasonable or unlawful. Examining the social parts of prize hunting reveals insight into the difficulties of offsetting social legacy with preservation objectives.

3. **Absence of Protection Mindfulness:**

In people group where protection mindfulness is low, people may accidentally add to poaching exercises. Lacking information about the biological significance of untamed life and the outcomes of poaching frustrates local area commitment in protection endeavors. Looking at the effect of mindfulness holes highlights the requirement for designated instruction and effort programs.

III. Powerless Administration and Policing:

1. **Defilement and Ineffectual Policing:**
Frail administration designs and debasement inside policing establish a climate helpful for poaching. The absence of responsibility and implementation components permits unlawful natural life exercises to prosper, as people might take advantage of escape clauses in the overall set of laws. Breaking down the job of debasement in poaching features the significance of reinforcing administration and policing.

2. **Lacking Punishments and Prevention:**
In locales where punishments for poaching are permissive, the discouragement impact is reduced, and people might be less reluctant to take part in unlawful untamed life exercises.
Analyzing the adequacy of punishments and discouragement estimates highlights the requirement for authoritative changes and the implementation of stricter punishments to battle poaching.

3. **Restricted Admittance to Equity:**

Networks with restricted admittance to equity might confront difficulties in detailing or tending to poaching occurrences. The shortfall of lawful response for impacted networks adds to a feeling of exemption for poachers. Breaking down the obstructions to get to equity accentuates the requirement for legitimate strengthening and local area based observing drives.

IV. Rivalry for Regular Assets:

1. **Land Use Clashes and Living space Infringement:**
   Contest for normal assets, especially land, can prompt contentions between natural life protection and human occupations. As people group grow their horticultural or touching regions, natural life environments recoil, increasing human-natural life clashes. Analyzing the effect of land use clashes on poaching inclusion highlights the significance of tending to contending interests through economical land the executives rehearses.

2. **Animals Predation and Retaliatory Killings:**
   In locales where natural life represents a danger to animals, networks might depend on retaliatory killings of hunters, including poaching exercises. Understanding the elements of human-natural life clashes features the interconnectedness of protection and work concerns. Executing moderation measures, for example, resistant to hunter fenced in areas, adds to compromise and diminishes the probability of retaliatory poaching.

3. **Asset Shortage and Poaching as a Step by step process for surviving:**

In regions with scant assets, people might go to poaching as a step by step process for surviving, taking advantage of untamed life for food, medication, or materials. Analyzing the effect of asset shortage on poaching highlights the significance of carrying out feasible asset the executives practices and elective occupation choices.

V. Local area Based Preservation Approaches:

1. **Boosting Preservation Practices:**
   Boosting preservation rehearses inside neighborhood networks can move the concentration from abuse to supportable conjunction with untamed life. Executing people group based motivation programs, for example, eco-the travel industry drives or income sharing systems, gives substantial advantages to networks participated in protection endeavors.

2. **Instruction and Mindfulness Projects:**
   Schooling and mindfulness programs assume a crucial part in changing mentalities towards untamed life and encouraging a feeling of obligation for protection. Designated outreach, school projects, and local area studios add to building a protection disapproved of local area. Dissecting the effect of schooling drives highlights the requirement for consistent mindfulness crusades.

3. **Local area Commitment in Preservation Direction:**

Enabling nearby networks to effectively take part in protection dynamic cycles cultivates a feeling of pride and obligation. Comprehensive administration models that include networks in natural life the board plans and navigation add to feasible preservation endeavors. Looking at fruitful local area commitment models advises the advancement regarding participatory methodologies.

VI. Practical Work Choices:

1. **Broadening of Vocations:**
   Tending to the financial drivers of poaching includes expanding work choices for nearby networks. Setting out open doors for practical horticulture, eco-accommodating ventures, and limited scope organizations decreases reliance on normal assets and mitigates neediness. Investigating effective vocation enhancement programs educates the plan regarding custom fitted drives for various settings.

2. **Ability Improvement and Limit Building:**
   Putting resources into expertise advancement and limit building programs upgrades the employability of local area individuals in non-manipulative areas. Furnishing people with attractive abilities diminishes their dependence on poaching as well as adds to the general advancement of the local area. Surveying the effect of limit building drives advises the versatility and maintainability regarding such projects.

3. **Elective Pay Age Undertakings:**

Carrying out elective pay age projects, like workmanship creation, agro-handling, or local area based the travel industry, gives feasible options in contrast to poaching. Analyzing effective undertakings features the potential for producing pay while advancing feasible practices and preservation mindfulness.

VII. Reinforcing Policing Administration:

1. **Against Defilement Measures:**
   Combatting defilement inside policing requires thorough enemy of debasement measures. Executing straightforward frameworks, informant insurances, and ordinary reviews add to establishing a climate of responsibility. Investigating the adequacy of against debasement measures illuminates procedures for reinforcing administration.

2. **Limit Working for Policing:**
   Building the limit of policing is fundamental for working on their viability in battling poaching. Preparing programs, furnishing staff with cutting edge innovation, and advancing cooperation with networks upgrade the capacity to implement untamed life insurance regulations. Surveying the effect of limit building drives illuminates continuous enhancements in policing.

3. **Lawful Changes and Punishments:**

Checking on and improving existing untamed life assurance regulations to guarantee stricter punishments for poaching is pivotal for discouragement. Dissecting the effect of lawful changes on poaching rates illuminates the continuous endeavors to make a legitimate structure that successfully shields untamed life.

4.2 The impact on the lives of rangers and conservationists

Officers and progressives assume a critical part in shielding the world's biodiversity, frequently confronting impressive difficulties and risking their lives to safeguard imperiled species and delicate environments. This paper investigates the significant effect on the existences of officers and traditionalists, revealing insight into the physical, close to home, and social parts of their devotion to natural protection.

1. **Actual Difficulties and Dangers:**
1. **Dangers of the Field:**
   Officers and progressives work in assorted and frequently brutal conditions, confronting actual difficulties that reach from outrageous weather patterns to rough landscapes. Whether watching thick woods, observing natural life in distant regions, or defying poachers, their work opens them to the components and stances intrinsic dangers to their actual prosperity.

2. **Untamed life Experiences:**
   Drawing in with wild creatures in their normal environments, while fundamental for preservation endeavors, presents huge dangers. Officers might experience regional creatures, defy perilous hunters, or end up in surprising, possibly hazardous circumstances.
   The need to adjust insurance and regard for natural life adds an additional layer of intricacy to their day to day undertakings.

3. **Poaching and Struggle Circumstances:**

The battle against poaching frequently places officers in head-to-head a conflict with equipped crooks. The unlawful natural life exchange is energized by strong crook organizations, and officers put their lives in extreme danger to check these illegal exercises. The danger of savagery and equipped struggle in districts with high biodiversity esteem further heightens the risks looked by those on the cutting edges of preservation.

II. Mental Cost:

1. **Injury and Stress:**
   The idea of protection work uncovered officers and moderates to horrible encounters, including seeing the consequence of poaching episodes, experiencing harmed creatures, or defying the annihilation of regular living spaces. These encounters add to elevated degrees of stress and close to home injury, affecting their psychological prosperity.

2. **Close to home Association with Untamed life:**
   Moderates frequently foster profound close to home associations with the

natural life they secure. Seeing the effect of poaching, living space misfortune, or environmental change on the species they treasure can prompt sensations of misery and powerlessness. The profound cost of seeing the downfall of species they have devoted their lives to shielding is a huge part of their work.

3. **Burnout and Psychological well-being Difficulties:**

The requesting and frequently unpleasant nature of protection work can prompt burnout and emotional wellness challenges among officers and preservationists. Extended periods, restricted assets, and the consistent fight against ecological dangers can add to pressure, nervousness, and misery. Tending to the emotional well-being requirements of those in the field is pivotal for supporting their obligation to protection.

III. Social Ramifications:

1. **Segregation and Restricted Assets:**
   Progressives frequently work in distant areas, prompting seclusion from family and social encouraging groups of people. Restricted admittance to assets, including clinical offices, instruction, and sporting exercises, further enhances the difficulties they face. The disconnection can influence their personal satisfaction and add to the intricacies of their work.

2. **Influence on Connections:**
   The requesting idea of protection work can strain individual connections. Officers and moderates might be expected to move habitually or burn through expanded periods from home, influencing their capacity to keep up with stable family lives. The stress on connections can be a huge penance for those devoted to natural safeguarding.

3. **Acknowledgment and Backing:**

Regardless of their fundamental job, officers and preservationists frequently work in the shadows, with restricted acknowledgment and backing. The absence of public mindfulness and comprehension of their commitments can prompt sensations of underappreciation and disappointment. Perceiving and esteeming their work is fundamental for supporting spirit and empowering supported responsibility.

IV. Proficient Turn of events:

1. **Preparing and Ability Upgrade:**
   Constant preparation and expertise improvement are pivotal for the adequacy of officers and protectionists. The unique idea of preservation work expects them to remain refreshed on the most recent advances, protection systems, and policing. Putting resources into their expert improvement guarantees they are better prepared to confront developing difficulties.

2. **Professional success Open doors:**
   Giving professional success open doors is fundamental for holding gifted and devoted people in the protection field. Perceiving their commitments through advancements, positions of authority, and open doors for specialization can upgrade work fulfillment and urge long haul obligation to protection endeavors.
3. **Local area Commitment and Strengthening:**

Integrating neighborhood networks into protection drives engages officers and progressives by cultivating cooperative endeavors. Building positive associations with networks, including them in dynamic cycles, and guaranteeing their prosperity adds to a more comprehensive and reasonable way to deal with preservation.

V. Protection Victories and Prizes:

1. **Species Recuperation and Natural surroundings Rebuilding:**
   Notwithstanding the difficulties, officers and progressives witness the positive effect of their endeavors, including fruitful species recuperations and natural surroundings reclamation. Praising these accomplishments builds up their feeling of direction and gives unmistakable proof of the meaning of their work.
2. **Local area Acknowledgment and Appreciation:**
   Expanding public mindfulness and appreciation for crafted by officers and moderates is crucial. Perceiving their commitments through grants, media inclusion, and local area affirmation can improve their confidence and move another age of ecological stewards.
3. **Worldwide Preservation Associations:**

Worldwide coordinated efforts and associations add to the progress of preservation drives. Interfacing officers and traditionalists to a worldwide organization encourages a feeling of fortitude and considers the sharing of information, assets, and best practices, at last reinforcing their effect on biodiversity protection.

4.3 Rise of organized crime and violence associated with rhino horn trade

The unlawful exchange rhino horns has turned into a worthwhile undertaking, driven by popularity in underground markets, especially in specific Asian nations where rhino horns are dishonestly accepted to have restorative properties. As the interest increments, so does the contribution of coordinated wrongdoing, prompting an ascent in viciousness related with the rhino horn exchange. This article investigates the disturbing heightening of coordinated wrongdoing and savagery in the unlawful exchange of rhino horns, analyzing the complex elements and their hindering effect on rhino populaces and worldwide protection endeavors.

1. **The Nexus Between Coordinated Wrongdoing and Rhino Horn Exchange:**

1. **Global Lawbreaker Organizations:**
   The rhino horn exchange has developed into a transnational criminal endeavor, with refined networks working across borders. Coordinated wrongdoing bunches are associated with each phase of the store network, from poaching and dealing to dispersion. The inclusion of these crook networks has raised the rhino horn exchange to a degree of refinement that represents an extreme danger to policing preservation endeavors.

2. **Defilement and Invasion:**
   Defilement inside policing, customs, and government authorities has worked with the exercises of coordinated wrongdoing in the rhino horn exchange. The invasion of degenerate people permits criminal organizations to work with relative exemption, sabotaging the viability of legitimate systems and authorization instruments.

3. **Tax evasion and Funding:**

The monstrous benefits created by the unlawful rhino horn exchange furnish criminal associations with significant assets. Tax evasion methods are utilized to legitimize these assets, making it provoking for specialists to follow and battle the monetary parts of the criminal venture. The implantation of unlawful assets further reinforces the functional limit of coordinated wrongdoing in the rhino horn exchange.

II. Brutality Related with Rhino Horn Dealing:

1. **Poaching-Related Brutality:**
   Poaching exercises are many times described by outrageous viciousness. Furnished poachers outfitted with modern weapons penetrate safeguarded regions, defy officers, and hardheartedly kill rhinos for their horns. The utilization of powerful weaponry imperils the existences of rhinos as well as represents a critical danger to the security of traditionalists and policing endeavoring to safeguard these jeopardized creatures.

2. **Furnished Struggle with Specialists:**
   As policing escalate endeavors to battle poaching, vicious conflicts among specialists and poachers have become progressively normal. The utilization of guns and the potential for equipped showdowns establish a perilous climate, heightening the gamble of wounds and fatalities on the two sides. Rhino insurance has coincidentally transformed into a landmark among progressives and very much furnished criminal components.

3. **Between Posse Viciousness:**

Rivalry among various crook networks associated with the rhino horn exchange can prompt between posse brutality. Clashes over regions, pirating courses, and control of key business sectors add to a pattern of brutality that further endangers rhino populaces and sabotages protection drives. The blow-back caused for networks trapped in the crossfire strengthens the negative social effect.

III. Influence on Rhino Populaces:

1. **Fast Decrease in Rhino Numbers:**
   The savagery related with the rhino horn exchange straightforwardly adds to the fast decrease in rhino populaces. Poaching, powered by coordinated wrongdoing, has arrived at unreasonable levels, driving a few rhino animal varieties to the edge of eradication. The deficiency of individual rhinos reduces hereditary variety as well as disturbs natural equilibrium in their living spaces.

2. **Interruption of Rearing and Social Designs:**
   The brutal idea of poaching upsets the normal reproducing and social designs of rhino populaces. The deficiency of key people, particularly mature rearing guys and females, prevents regenerative achievement. The subsequent disturbance in friendly orders can have flowing impacts, affecting the general wellbeing and flexibility of rhino networks.

3. **Preservation Difficulties and Asset Redirection:**

The ascent of coordinated wrongdoing and brutality puts extra weights on protection associations and specialists. Assets that could be dispensed to fundamental preservation exercises, like natural surroundings insurance and local area commitment, are redirected to battle the raising danger of crimes. This redirection subverts more extensive protection objectives and debilitates the general reaction to the rhino horn exchange.

IV. Global Reaction and Countermeasures:

1. **Fortifying Policing Cooperation:**
   Tending to the coordinated wrongdoing related with the rhino horn exchange requires a purposeful global exertion. Fortifying policing, upgrading coordinated effort among nations, and executing knowledge sharing components are essential moves toward disturbing crook organizations and diminishing the commonness of brutality.

2. **Public Mindfulness and Request Decrease:**
   Instructing people in general about the deceptions encompassing the restorative properties of rhino horns is fundamental for diminishing interest. Global missions to bring issues to light about the outcomes of rhino poaching and the related savagery can add to a change in cultural perspectives and lessening the interest for rhino horn items.

3. **Local area Commitment and Against Debasement Measures:**

Including neighborhood networks in protection endeavors and carrying out enemy of debasement measures are crucial parts of combatting coordinated wrongdoing in the rhino horn exchange. Enabling people group to oppose association in poaching exercises, giving elective livelihoods, and guaranteeing the fair appropriation of advantages from preservation endeavors are key procedures.

Chapter 5

Socioeconomic Ramifications

Rhino horn dealing, driven by request in different business sectors, has sweeping financial results that stretch out past the quick effect on rhino populaces. This paper investigates the complex financial consequences of rhino horn dealing, inspecting what this unlawful exchange means for networks, economies, and the general prosperity of social orders. From the nearby level to the worldwide stage, understanding these implications is fundamental for creating successful methodologies to battle the unlawful exchange and address its hidden drivers.

1. **Nearby People group and Vocations:**
1. **Financial Reliance on Poaching:**
   In districts where rhino populaces are found, nearby networks might turn out to be monetarily subject to poaching exercises. The charm of easy gains from the unlawful exchange can make a pattern of reliance, subverting practical financial turn of events. The financial texture of these networks is trapped with poaching, prompting long haul ramifications for the two people and the local area all in all.
2. **Neediness and Absence of Elective Occupations:**
   Rhino poaching frequently flourishes in regions with elevated degrees of neediness and restricted admittance to elective occupations. The shortfall of feasible monetary open doors prompts people to take part in criminal operations for monetary endurance. Tending to the financial underlying drivers, like destitution and absence of work, is pivotal for breaking the pattern of reliance on rhino horn dealing.
3. **Interruption of Conventional Ways of life:**

The convergence of criminal operations related with rhino horn dealing can disturb customary ways of life of nearby networks. Expanded contribution in poaching might prompt a shift away from reasonable works on, changing the social and social elements that have molded these networks for ages.

II. Preservation Subsidizing and Asset Allotment:

1. **Redirection of Preservation Assets:**
   The illegal exchange rhino horns redirects significant preservation assets from basic drives pointed toward safeguarding natural life and their territories.
   Reserves that could be allotted to hostile to poaching endeavors, natural surroundings conservation, and local area commitment are diverted to battle the lawbreaker networks associated with rhino horn dealing. This redirection hampers the general viability of protection systems.
2. **Monetary Burden on Preservation Associations:**
   Protection associations face monetary strain because of the raising difficulties presented by rhino horn dealing. The requirement for expanded safety efforts, innovation, and staff to battle poaching puts a significant weight on the monetary assets of these associations. The constant weapons contest among moderates and poachers further compounds the stress on restricted reserves.
3. **Influence on Worldwide Preservation Drives:**

The worldwide preservation local area is impacted by the financial implications of rhino horn dealing. The assets expected to battle natural life wrongdoing could some way or another be utilized for more extensive preservation drives tending to environmental change, biodiversity misfortune, and the assurance of different jeopardized species. The redirection of consideration and assets to address the quick danger of rhino poaching has more extensive ramifications for worldwide preservation endeavors.

III. The travel industry and Ecotourism:

1. **Decrease in Vacation destinations:**
   The flourishing untamed life and biodiversity of locales with rhino populaces are many times key vacation spots. The danger presented by rhino horn dealing to these magnetic megafauna can possibly lessen the allure of these areas for ecotourism. A decrease in traveler visits adversely influences neighborhood economies that depend on the travel industry income.
2. **Financial Effect on Friendliness and Administration Areas:**
   Rhino-related ecotourism creates pay and work amazing open doors in the friendliness and administration areas. The decrease in vacationer numbers because of worries over rhino poaching influences organizations like lodgings, eateries, and visit administrators, prompting financial difficulties for networks reliant upon these enterprises.
3. **Potential for Supportable The travel industry:**

Combatting rhino horn dealing and guaranteeing the security of rhino populaces can add to the improvement of feasible the travel industry models. By accentuating protection endeavors, dependable the travel industry, and local area commitment, districts can remake their allure as objections for cognizant voyagers, encouraging long haul financial supportability.

IV. Global Exchange and Strategic Relations:

1. **Conciliatory Pressures and Exchange Limitations:**
   The unlawful exchange rhino horns can strain conciliatory relations between nations engaged with the market interest chains. Nations where rhinos are poached may confront worldwide strain to upgrade against poaching measures, while those with interest for rhino items might encounter exchange limitations and discretionary pressures. These issues have more extensive ramifications for worldwide collaboration on ecological and protection matters.

2. **Transnational Wrongdoing and Collaboration:**
   Rhino horn dealing is a transnational wrongdoing that requires worldwide co-operation for powerful arrangements. The illegal exchange network frequently ranges numerous nations, and tending to the main drivers requests a unified front. Challenges in cultivating participation might emerge because of clashing public interests, making it basic to assemble agreement on combatting natural life wrongdoing.

3. **Worldwide Discernments and Notoriety:**

Nations embroiled in rhino horn dealing can confront reputational harm on the worldwide stage. The association of nationals or substances in the unlawful exchange might discolor the worldwide standing of these nations. Unfriendly discernments can influence discretionary relations as well as the travel industry, unfamiliar venture, and cooperation in worldwide preservation drives.

V. Security and Strength:

1. **Militarization of Protection Regions:**
   The ascent of coordinated wrongdoing and savagery related with rhino horn dealing frequently prompts the militarization of protection regions. Expanded safety efforts, including the organization of military, might be important to counter exceptional poaching organizations. While these actions plan to safe-guard untamed life, they can likewise raise worries about denials of basic liberties and compound strains in neighborhood networks.

2. **Destabilization of Locales:**
   Locales with elevated degrees of rhino poaching might encounter destabilization because of the presence of criminal organizations. The flood of unlawful assets, defilement, and savagery related with rhino horn dealing can add to more exten-sive issues of administration, security, and social soundness. The destabilization

of areas further muddles protection endeavors and compromises generally local security.

3. **Social Struggle and Local area Division:**

Networks situated in or close to rhino living spaces might encounter unseen fits of turmoil and divisions because of rhino poaching. The financial motivations related with poaching can make strains among local area individuals, prompting social clash. Tending to these divisions is fundamental for building a unified front against poaching and encouraging local area driven protection endeavors.

VI. Legitimate and Administrative Structures:

1. **Deficiency of Lawful Hindrances:**
   The financial consequences of rhino horn dealing with are exacerbated by insufficiencies lawful obstructions. The punishments for participating in unlawful natural life exchange may not be comparable with the expected benefits, making it a generally okay, high-reward movement. Reinforcing lawful systems and forcing stricter punishments are fundamental for deflecting people and criminal organizations engaged with rhino horn dealing.

2. **Debasement and Requirement Difficulties:**
   Debasement inside lawful and implementation frameworks represents a huge test in combatting rhino horn dealing. The inclusion of degenerate authorities permits criminal organizations to work with relative exemption. Tending to debasement and improving implementation limits are basic parts of making a powerful lawful obstruction against rhino poaching.

3. **Worldwide Collaboration in Legitimate Measures:**

Orchestrating legitimate structures and advancing worldwide collaboration in lawful measures are significant for battling rhino horn dealing. Steady and tough regulations across nations engaged with the organic market chains can make a bound together front against the unlawful exchange. Creating viable legitimate systems requires joint effort and responsibility at the worldwide level.

5.1 Economic impact on countries with rhino populations

Nations favored with rhino populaces frequently end up at the crossing point of biodiversity protection and financial turn of events. The presence of these notable species adds to the natural wealth of these countries, making them important resources for the travel industry and potential exploration valuable open doors. Be that as it may, the financial effect on nations with rhino populaces is an intricate scene impacted by different elements, including the preservation endeavors expected to safeguard these jeopardized species, the difficulties presented by poaching, and the possible advantages from dependable the travel industry.

This exposition investigates the diverse financial components of nations with rhino populaces, looking at how the preservation of rhinos converges with more extensive monetary contemplations.

1. **Biodiversity and Ecotourism:**
1. **Worth of Rhinos in Ecotourism:**
Nations with rhino populaces frequently influence the presence of these lofty animals for ecotourism, drawing in guests excited about encountering untamed life right at home. The financial worth of rhinos reaches out past the actual creatures to the biological systems they possess. Safari visits, natural life photography, and rhino-driven encounters add to the travel industry, creating income for nearby networks and public economies.

2. **Financial Commitments from Traveler Spending:**
Traveler spending on rhino-related exercises, including park section charges, directed visits, and convenience, infuses income into neighborhood economies. The financial advantages stretch out to a scope of administrations, like transportation, cordiality, and neighborhood organizations. Subsequently, the travel industry area turns into a vital driver of monetary development, giving immediate and backhanded business potential open doors for networks encompassing rhino environments.

3. **Feasible The travel industry Models:**

Creating feasible the travel industry models that focus on capable and moral practices is fundamental for augmenting the monetary advantages of rhino populaces. Adjusting the inundation of vacationers with protection needs guarantees that the monetary effect is positive, supporting both neighborhood jobs and the drawn out conservation of rhino environments.

II. Protection Expenses and Ventures:

1. **Monetary Responsibilities to Hostile to Poaching Measures:**
Nations with rhino populaces face significant monetary responsibilities to counter the danger of poaching. The ascent of coordinated wrongdoing networks engaged with rhino horn dealing with requires expanded speculations against poaching measures. These uses cover gear, innovation, work force, and preparing expected to shield rhinos from criminal operations.

2. **Preservation Associations and Subsidizing:**
Preservation associations assume a vital part in supporting nations with rhino populaces. Worldwide and neighborhood elements contribute financing, ability, and assets to support preservation endeavors.
Monetary help is coordinated towards environment security, local area

commitment, research drives, and hostile to poaching exercises, assisting nations with exploring the intricate difficulties related with rhino preservation.

3. **Offsetting Protection Expenses with Financial Turn of events:**

Finding a sensitive harmony between the expenses of rhino protection and more extensive financial improvement objectives is really difficult for nations with rhino populaces. While interests in preservation are basic for the endurance of these species, legislatures should gauge these consumptions against other squeezing financial needs, like medical care, schooling, and foundation improvement.

III. Influence on Neighborhood People group:

1. **Local area Based Protection Drives:**
   Integrating neighborhood networks into preservation drives is critical for guaranteeing that financial advantages are conveyed evenhandedly. Local area based preservation models enable nearby occupants to partake in rhino security endeavors effectively. This commitment can prompt business amazing open doors, ability improvement, and income sharing systems that straightforwardly benefit those living in closeness to rhino territories.

2. **Maintainable Occupation Options:**
   Nations with rhino populaces should investigate maintainable occupation options for neighborhood networks. Enhancing pay sources through drives like agro-the travel industry, craftsmanship creation, and practical agribusiness can lessen reliance on rhino-related exercises and give monetary strength to networks impacted by protection endeavors.

3. **Tending to Human-Untamed life Struggle:**

Rhino preservation can accidentally add to human-untamed life clashes as these creatures navigate domains close to human settlements. The financial effect on neighborhood networks incorporates possible harm to crops, domesticated animals predation, and wellbeing concerns. Carrying out techniques to moderate these contentions, for example, the improvement of hunter resistant nooks, guarantees that financial misfortunes are limited.

IV. Global Coordinated effort and Subsidizing:

1. **Worldwide Protection Associations:**
   Nations with rhino populaces frequently benefit from worldwide protection associations. Cooperative endeavors with global associations, non-benefits, and contributor nations give monetary help, specialized mastery, and exploration support. These associations reinforce the limit of nations to handle the diverse difficulties of rhino preservation.

2. **Subsidizing Difficulties and Reliance:**
   While worldwide subsidizing is urgent for rhino preservation, nations should be careful about turning out to be excessively reliant upon outer help. Overreliance on unfamiliar financing might subvert nearby responsibility for endeavors and compromise the manageability of drives. Nations need to foster systems for steadily diminishing reliance on outside subsidizing while at the same time encouraging homegrown interest in protection.

3. **Research and Logical Joint effort:**

Rhino populaces offer remarkable open doors for logical examination, adding to how we might interpret biodiversity, environments, and creature conduct. Cooperative exploration drives including nearby and worldwide researchers upgrade the logical information base and set out open doors for instructive and research establishments inside nations with rhino populaces.

V. Financial Capability of Rhino Horns:

1. **Lawful Exchange Contemplations:**
   The likely financial worth of rhino horns represents a complex moral situation. While sanctioning the exchange rhino horns could produce income for preservation, worries about propagating request, empowering criminal operations, and moral contemplations make this a quarrelsome issue. Nations should cautiously think about the monetary advantages in contrast to the expected dangers and moral ramifications of sanctioning the exchange.

2. **Creative Subsidizing Models:**
   Investigating creative subsidizing models can assist nations with opening monetary potential without turning to the exchange rhino horns. Models, for example, protection securities, eco-accommodating confirmations, and organizations with private undertakings can give practical subsidizing streams to rhino preservation while keeping away from the adverse results related with the exchange.

3. **Monetary Strength through Enhancement:**

Expanding monetary procedures past the possible worth of rhino horns is urgent for long haul flexibility. Nations with rhino populaces ought to investigate elective income streams, for example, carbon offset programs, biodiversity balances, and practical asset the board, to guarantee monetary soundness free of the dubious exchange rhino horns.

VI. Environmental Change Versatility:

1. **Biological system Administrations and Environment Moderation:**
   Rhino environments assume a critical part in giving biological system administrations, including carbon sequestration and environment guideline. The

conservation of these environments adds to environmental change relief endeavors. The financial worth of unblemished environments stretches out past direct income age, as solid biological systems offer fundamental types of assistance for horticulture, water supply, and environment strength.

2. **Monetary Advantages of Biological Wellbeing:**
Keeping up with the environmental wellbeing of rhino territories offers financial advantages past the quick extent of protection. Solid environments support agribusiness, water assets, and biodiversity, adding to the general prosperity of social orders. The financial flexibility of nations with rhino populaces is unpredictably connected to the wellbeing and imperativeness of their indigenous habitats.

3. **Environment Related Dangers to Rhino Living spaces:**

Environmental change presents huge dangers to rhino natural surroundings, remembering shifts for vegetation designs, adjusted water accessibility, and expanded recurrence of outrageous climate occasions. Moderating these environment related gambles requires proactive protection measures and versatile procedures to guarantee the drawn out reasonability of rhino populaces and the biological systems they occupy.

5.2 The role of corruption in exacerbating the issue

Defilement is an unavoidable and slippery power that subverts endeavors to address different cultural difficulties, remembering the illegal exchange for rhino horns. The association of degenerate practices at numerous levels of the store network, from poaching to dealing, altogether compounds the issue of rhino horn dealing. This exposition digs into the complex ways defilement adds to the issue, inspecting its effect on policing, systems, and global cooperation. Understanding the job of defilement is critical for creating viable procedures to battle rhino horn dealing and safeguard these jeopardized species.

1. **Defilement in Poaching Exercises:**
1. **Invasion of Untamed life Security Organizations:**
Defilement frequently invades natural life assurance offices, compromising the very foundations answerable for defending rhinos. Poachers exploit degenerate authorities to acquire data about watch courses, safety efforts, and weak rhino populaces. The invasion of policing debilitates the ability to counter poaching exercises and permits crooks to work without any potential repercussions.

2. **Pay off and Insider Data:**
Debasement in poaching exercises much of the time includes pay off and the trading of insider data. Poachers might pay off park officers, guides, or other staff with information on rhino areas and watch plans. This insider data empowers poachers to dodge safety efforts, making it simpler to find and target rhinos for their horns.

3. **Shortcomings in Policing:**

Debasement inside policing makes shortcomings in the general reaction to rhino horn dealing. The absence of successful examinations, captures, and indictments because of degenerate practices hampers endeavors to destroy poaching organizations. The abuse of legitimate provisos and the assurance of people associated with the unlawful exchange propagate the pattern of debasement and untamed life wrongdoing.

II. Debasement in Lawful Structures:

1. **Regulation and Administrative Holes:**
   Defilement flourishes in conditions where lawful structures are feeble or deficiently authorized. Nations with deficient regulation, administrative holes, or remiss requirement instruments become focal points for degenerate practices connected with rhino horn dealing. The shortfall of rigid legitimate hindrances permits the illegal exchange to thrive, subverting preservation endeavors.

2. **Administrative Catch:**
   Administrative catch happens when people or substances inside administrative bodies focus on private interests over their authority obligations. With regards to rhino horn dealing, administrative catch can prompt the control of grants, licenses, and amounts. Degenerate authorities might work with the lawful exchange rhino horns or choose to disregard infringement, adding to the general test of battling unlawful exchange.

3. **Legitimate Protections and Abuse:**

Degenerate practices reach out to lawful safeguards and escape clauses that dealers exploit to avoid equity. Legitimate experts, including attorneys and judges, might be powerless to pay off or pressure, bringing about ideal results for people engaged with rhino horn dealing. The control of lawful cycles subverts the viability of legitimate measures against untamed life wrongdoing.

III. Debasement in Global Joint effort:

1. **Cross-Boundary Dealing and Complicity:**
   The worldwide idea of rhino horn dealing requires global joint effort to battle the issue successfully. Notwithstanding, debasement can impede such joint effort when authorities in a single nation are complicit in or benefit from the exercises of dealers. Cross-line dealing turns out to be more difficult to address when debasement works with the development of illegal merchandise across borders.

2. **Strategic and Political Impacts:**
   Defilement can stretch out to strategic and political circles, impacting the needs and activities of legislatures. Nations with critical interest for rhino horns might apply discretionary tension or utilize degenerate practices to impact source nations to take on arrangements that line up with their monetary advantages. This

powerful hampers the advancement of peaceful accords and helpful endeavors to battle natural life wrongdoing.

3. **Illegal tax avoidance and Unlawful Funds:**

Defilement works with tax evasion and the progression of illegal funds related with rhino horn dealing. Criminal organizations exploit feeble monetary guidelines, complicit banks, and degenerate authorities to legitimize the returns from criminal operations. The cross-line nature of monetary exchanges connected with rhino horn dealing requires strong worldwide cooperation to follow and upset illegal monetary streams.

IV. Influences on Preservation Endeavors:

1. **Disintegration of Confidence in Preservation Organizations:**
   Debasement disintegrates trust in protection organizations, both locally and universally. At the point when networks see that protection endeavors are undermined by defilement, their eagerness to take part in preservation drives decreases. Building trust is fundamental for encouraging local area association and backing for rhino protection.

2. **Redirection of Protection Assets:**
   Defilement redirects important assets from basic preservation drives. Reserves reserved for hostile to poaching endeavors, natural surroundings security, and local area commitment might be redirected through degenerate practices. The redirection of assets debilitates the general limit of protection associations and states to address the main drivers of rhino horn dealing.

3. **Shortcomings in Protection Methodologies:**

Defilement presents shortcomings in protection techniques by sabotaging the viability of against poaching measures and local area commitment programs. Preservationists might confront obstruction or detachment from neighborhood networks suspicious of degenerate foundations. This subverts the cooperative endeavors vital for maintainable preservation.

V. Tending to Defilement in Rhino Horn Dealing:

1. **Fortifying Lawful Structures and Requirement:**
   Reinforcing legitimate structures and requirement systems is fundamental for tending to debasement in rhino horn dealing. Nations should institute and uphold rigid regulations with serious punishments for untamed life wrongdoing. Standard reviews, straightforward detailing, and autonomous oversight can help distinguish and correct degenerate practices inside preservation establishments.

2. **Upgrading Worldwide Cooperation:**
   Global coordinated effort is fundamental for tending to the transnational idea

of rhino horn dealing. Cooperation should reach out past policing incorporate strategic endeavors, insight sharing, and limit building drives. Laying out and sticking to global principles for fighting defilement in the natural life exchange is significant for cultivating collaboration.

3. **Local area Strengthening and Training:**
Enabling neighborhood networks and bringing issues to light about the effect of defilement on protection endeavors are essential parts of battling rhino horn dealing. Local area based programs that give elective livelihoods, schooling, and limit building open doors can lessen weakness to debasement and upgrade local area support for protection.

4. **Advancing Informant Insurances:**
Making powerful informant insurance systems is vital for empowering people inside protection establishments and policing to report defilement unafraid of counter. Informants assume a basic part in uncovering degenerate practices and considering people responsible for their activities.

5. **Using Innovation for Straightforwardness:**

Utilizing innovation, for example, blockchain and secure data sets, can upgrade straightforwardness in protection endeavors. Straightforward record-keeping of grants, exchanges, and implementation activities can lessen open doors for defilement. Furthermore, the utilization of innovation in checking and reconnaissance can support hostile to poaching endeavors.

5.3 Global economic implications of illegal wildlife trade

The unlawful untamed life exchange has critical and extensive financial ramifications on a worldwide scale. Past the prompt dangers to biodiversity and preservation endeavors, the financial effect traverses different areas, influencing networks, economies, and global relations. This exposition investigates the complex associations between unlawful natural life exchange and the worldwide economy, revealing insight into the secret emergency that imperils natural life as well as the prosperity of social orders around the world.

1. **Loss of Biodiversity and Environment Administrations:**
1. **Financial Worth of Biodiversity:**
Biodiversity isn't just fundamental for the soundness of biological systems yet in addition holds impressive financial worth. The deficiency of assorted plant and creature species because of unlawful natural life exchange disturbs biological systems, prompting diminished strength to ecological changes. This, thusly, influences horticulture, fisheries, and different businesses reliant upon steady and working environments.

2. **Disturbance of Biological system Administrations:**

Environment administrations, like fertilization, water cleansing, and infection guideline, contribute altogether to the worldwide economy. The unlawful natural life exchange, by draining key species, upsets these administrations. This interruption has flowing impacts on agribusiness, human wellbeing, and the general limit of biological systems to give fundamental assets and administrations.

II. Monetary Effect on Neighborhood People group:

1. **Reliance on Untamed life Related Exercises:**
   In numerous areas, neighborhood networks rely upon natural life related exercises for their jobs. Lawful untamed life the travel industry, supportable hunting, and eco-accommodating artworks create pay and work open doors.
   The unlawful exchange undermines these exercises by exhausting natural life populaces, prompting monetary difficulties for networks subject to the feasible utilization of natural life assets.

2. **Loss of The travel industry Income:**
   Untamed life, including notable species designated by unlawful exchange, frequently fills in as a critical fascination for vacationers. The decrease in untamed life populaces because of poaching and dealing adversely influences the travel industry income. Nations that depend on untamed life based the travel industry experience monetary difficulties as the appeal of their regular marvels lessens.

3. **Debilitating of Social Texture:**

The unlawful untamed life exchange can add to the debilitating of social texture inside networks. Financial abberations, loss of customary vocations, and social struggles emerging from the unlawful exchange disturb local area attachment. This social shakiness further entangles endeavors to address the underlying drivers of natural life wrongdoing and advance supportable turn of events.

III. Worldwide Exchange and Monetary Organizations:

1. **Influence on Legitimate Untamed life Exchange:**
   Unlawful natural life exchange invades and subverts legitimate channels, influencing worldwide exchange elements. The presence of illegally obtained untamed life items in the market twists costs and rivals lawful other options. This has monetary ramifications for lawful ventures associated with the creation, deal, and exchange of natural life related items.

2. **Dangers to Human Wellbeing and Farming:**
   The unlawful natural life exchange presents dangers to human wellbeing and horticulture, with possible financial repercussions. Zoonotic illnesses sent through natural life dealing can prompt pandemics, upsetting economies and stressing medical care frameworks. Also, the presentation of intrusive species

through the exchange can have extreme ramifications for horticulture and bio-diversity.

3. **Monetary Effect of Policing:**

States and policing bear significant monetary costs in fighting unlawful natural life exchange. Interests in staff, innovation, and foundation to counter poaching and dealing redirect assets from other major problems. The monetary weight of upholding hostile to untamed life wrongdoing estimates highlights the complex idea of the test.

IV. Monetary Effect on Feasible Advancement Objectives:

1. **Subverting Reasonable Turn of events:**
   Unlawful natural life exchange straightforwardly sabotages a few Manageable Improvement Objectives (SDGs). The deficiency of biodiversity, financial im-balances, and social unsteadiness brought about by the unlawful exchange upset progress towards accomplishing SDGs connected with ecological maintainabil-ity, destitution annihilation, and local area prosperity.

2. **Influence on Worldwide Ventures:**
   Financial backers and monetary organizations are progressively perceiving the material dangers related with natural debasement and biodiversity misfortune. The unlawful untamed life exchange adds to these dangers, possibly influencing speculation choices. Organizations with supply anchors connected to untamed life related items might confront reputational harm, administrative investiga-tion, and monetary misfortunes.

3. **Amazing open doors for Economical Other options:**

Tending to the monetary effect of unlawful natural life exchange includes recogniz-ing and advancing practical other options. Interests in eco-accommodating the travel industry, preservation arranged ventures, and moral natural life related enterprises can add to financial advancement while saving biodiversity.

Chapter 6

International Response

Unlawful untamed life exchange represents a worldwide danger that requires composed global endeavors to battle. The reaction to this complicated issue includes discretionary coordinated effort, legitimate systems, requirement procedures, and local area commitment. This paper investigates the development of the global reaction to unlawful untamed life exchange, analyzing the difficulties confronted and the potential open doors for additional viable and economical arrangements.

1. **Authentic Outline of Global Reaction:**
1. **Early Acknowledgment and Preservation Arrangements:**
   The worldwide local area's attention to the effect of natural life exchange on biodiversity traces all the way back to the mid twentieth hundred years. The downfall of famous species, like the African elephant, provoked early protection endeavors. The marking of the Show for the Security of Fauna and Vegetation in 1933 established the groundwork for worldwide participation in tending to the unreasonable abuse of untamed life.
2. **Refers to and Administrative Systems:**
   The Show on Global Exchange Jeopardized Types of Wild Fauna and Vegetation (Refers to), laid out in 1973, arose as a milestone peaceful accord. Refers to expected to direct and screen the worldwide exchange of jeopardized species, putting limitations on the development of natural life items across borders. The show gave a legitimate system to nations to team up in controlling the exchange of undermined and imperiled species.
3. **Development of Worldwide Collaboration:**

Throughout the long term, global collaboration on unlawful natural life exchange developed to envelop a more extensive scope of partners. The Assembled Countries (UN), Interpol, and different associations became involved, perceiving the transnational idea of natural life wrongdoing. The reception of Supportable Advancement

Objectives (SDGs) in 2015 further coordinated untamed life preservation into the worldwide plan, underlining the interconnectedness of biodiversity and practical turn of events.

II. Challenges in the Worldwide Reaction:

1. **Implementation Holes and Shortcomings:**
   Upholding peaceful accords and public regulations stays a critical test in the battle against unlawful natural life exchange. Holes in implementation limits, defilement inside policing, and the absence of assets ruin the capacity to battle modern and all around financed criminal organizations. The difference in requirement capacities among nations further compounds the difficulties.

2. **Lawful Structure Variations:**
   Abberations in lawful structures and punishments across nations make provisos that dealers exploit. A few countries might have careless guidelines or restricted punishments for natural life wrongdoings, giving places of refuge to unlawful exercises. Blending legitimate structures worldwide is a complicated errand, requiring political discussions and shared obligation to combatting untamed life wrongdoing.

3. **Transnational Nature of Untamed life Wrongdoing:**
   The transnational idea of untamed life wrongdoing presents difficulties to coordination and data dividing between nations. Criminal organizations frequently exploit jurisdictional limits, making it challenging for policing to actually seek after examinations. Fortifying cross-line participation is basic to destroy dealing organizations and address the main drivers of unlawful exchange.

4. **Debasement and Administration:**
   Debasement inside nations ensnared in unlawful untamed life exchange subverts the viability of global endeavors. From pay off of policing to complicit government specialists, debasement encourages a climate where criminal organizations can work without any potential repercussions. Tending to debasement requires lawful measures as well as drives to improve administration and advance straightforwardness.

5. **Request Side Difficulties:**

While much spotlight is put on the inventory side of unlawful natural life exchange, tending to request side difficulties stays basic. Nations with popularity for untamed life items, especially in Asia, represent a huge snag to protection endeavors. Social convictions, conventional medication rehearses, and an absence of mindfulness add to the industriousness of interest, requiring designated schooling and mindfulness crusades.

III. Multilateral Drives and Associations:

1. **UNODC and Natural life Wrongdoing:**
   The Unified Countries Office on Medications and Wrongdoing (UNODC) plays had a critical impact in tending to natural life wrongdoing. Perceiving the nexus between natural life wrongdoing and different types of transnational coordinated wrongdoing, UNODC gives specialized help, limit building, and coordination to nations trying to battle unlawful untamed life exchange. The UNODC's work supplements more extensive endeavors to reinforce law and order and administration.

2. **INTERPOL's Job in Untamed life Wrongdoing:**
   INTERPOL, the Global Lawbreaker Police Association, works with worldwide police participation in battling untamed life wrongdoing. The association gives a protected stage to part nations to share data, insight, and best practices. INTER-POL's Natural Security Program centers around building the limit of policing to address unlawful untamed life exchange and related ecological wrongdoings.

3. **The Worldwide Climate Office (GEF):**

The Worldwide Climate Office, a monetary component for ecological shows, upholds projects pointed toward tending to unlawful untamed life exchange. The GEF finances drives that attention on reinforcing lawful systems, improving implementation capacities, and advancing economical choices for networks impacted by natural life wrongdoing.

IV. Lawful Instruments and Arrangements:

1. **Refers to and Revisions:**
   Refers to keeps on being a foundation of global endeavors to direct untamed life exchange. The show intermittently surveys and updates its reference sections to mirror the changing status of species. Ongoing corrections to Refers to have included measures to address arising difficulties, for example, the guideline of online untamed life exchange and the consideration of extra species under insurance.

2. **The UN Show Against Transnational Coordinated Wrongdoing:**
   The UN Show Against Transnational Coordinated Wrongdoing, otherwise called the Palermo Show, incorporates conventions that address different types of coordinated wrongdoing, including natural life dealing. The Convention against the Illegal Assembling of and Dealing with Guns, Their Parts and Parts and Ammo (Guns Convention) has suggestions for fighting the unlawful weapons exchange frequently connected to untamed life wrongdoing.

3. **Territorial Arrangements:**

Territorial arrangements have demonstrated successful in encouraging joint effort among adjoining nations. For instance, the ASEAN Untamed life Requirement

Organization (ASEAN-WEN) unites Southeast Asian countries to battle natural life dealing. Local coordinated efforts take into consideration more designated reactions, sharing of knowledge, and joint activities to disturb criminal organizations working across borders.

V. Monetary Systems and Motivating forces:

1. **The Monetary Activity Team (FATF):**
   The Monetary Activity Team, an intergovernmental association zeroed in on battling tax evasion and psychological oppressor supporting, has perceived the connection between monetary violations and natural life dealing. Nations are urged to consider the monetary parts of untamed life wrongdoing in their gamble evaluations and execute measures to distinguish and forestall illegal monetary streams related with the exchange.

2. **Monetary Impetuses for Preservation:**
   Advancing monetary impetuses for preservation is a significant part of the worldwide reaction. Drives that perceive the worth of flawless biological systems and biodiversity add to maintainable turn of events. Installments for biological system administrations, eco-the travel industry, and affirmation projects can give monetary options that decrease dependence on the abuse of natural life.

3. **Confidential Area Commitment:**

Drawing in the confidential area is progressively perceived as fundamental in the battle against unlawful untamed life exchange. Organizations engaged with transportation, web based business, and the travel industry can assume a part in forestalling the dealing of untamed life items. Cooperative endeavors between legislatures, NGOs, and organizations can improve inventory network straightforwardness and dependable strategic approaches.

VI. Local area Commitment and Strengthening:

1. **Engaging Neighborhood People group:**
   Perceiving the job of neighborhood networks in untamed life protection is basic. Enabling people group to be stewards of their normal assets includes giving elective occupations, schooling, and open doors for economical turn of events. Local area commitment encourages a feeling of pride over protection endeavors, making networks partners in the battle against unlawful natural life exchange.

2. **Native Information and Practices:**
   Recognizing and consolidating native information and practices is fundamental in making viable protection procedures. Native people group frequently have conventional biological information that can add to natural life preservation. Regarding and coordinating these practices into preservation drives upgrades the viability of endeavors as well as advances social variety.

3. **Global Guide and Improvement Help:**

Worldwide guide and improvement help assume a huge part in supporting nations impacted by unlawful untamed life exchange. Interests in training, medical services, and framework can add to tending to the financial variables that drive networks toward impractical double-dealing of untamed life. Fitting help to explicit requirements and encouraging nearby responsibility for drives is pivotal.

VII. Mechanical Developments and Apparatuses:

1. **Natural life Crime scene investigation and DNA Examination:**
   Mechanical progressions in natural life criminology and DNA examination have become useful assets in the battle against unlawful untamed life exchange. These strategies empower specialists to follow the beginning of held onto untamed life items, recognize poaching areas of interest, and fabricate arguments against dealers. The utilization of state of the art innovation upgrades policing and fills in as a hindrance to would-be dealers.

2. **Satellite Following and Checking:**
   Satellite following and checking frameworks offer continuous information on untamed life developments and territory changes. Incorporating satellite innovation into preservation endeavors considers more successful enemy of poaching tasks and the assurance of basic environments. Observing frameworks likewise add to knowledge gathering, helping policing disturbing dealing organizations.

3. **Advanced Stages and Network protection:**

The ascent of online natural life dealing has required endeavors to battle unlawful exchange on computerized stages. Fortifying network protection measures, cooperation with web based business organizations, and utilizing innovation to screen online commercial centers are pivotal in tending to the difficulties presented by the advanced component of unlawful untamed life exchange.

VIII. Public Mindfulness and Schooling:

1. **Mindfulness Missions and Schooling:**
   Public mindfulness missions and instruction programs are fundamental parts of the global reaction. Expanding mindfulness about the results of unlawful untamed life exchange, the effect on biodiversity, and the job of people in forestalling request helps shift cultural perspectives. Training drives can target both shopper nations and source nations, encouraging a worldwide comprehension of the significance of natural life protection.

2. **Big name and Force to be reckoned with Commitment:**
   Drawing in VIPs and powerhouses can enhance mindfulness missions and contact a more extensive crowd. Well known individuals who advocate for natural

life preservation point out the issue, empowering social change and affecting general assessment. Key organizations with powerhouses can use their foundation to pass on protection messages successfully.

3. **Dependable The travel industry and Purchaser Decisions:**

Advancing dependable the travel industry and purchaser decisions adds to lessening interest for natural life items. Explorers can pick natural life well disposed the travel industry administrators, and purchasers can pursue informed decisions to stay away from items related with unlawful exchange. Dependable way of behaving by people and organizations is a strong power in molding market elements and advancing moral practices.

IX. Arising Patterns and Future Difficulties:

1. **Developing Nature of Untamed life Wrongdoing:**
The unlawful untamed life exchange keeps on developing, introducing new difficulties for the global local area. The development of online stages, the utilization of refined dealing courses, and the contribution of coordinated wrongdoing networks require continuous transformation of systems and cooperation among nations and associations.

2. **Environmental Change and Living space Misfortune:**
Environmental change and natural surroundings misfortune further confound endeavors to battle unlawful untamed life exchange. Changes in environment designs, loss of natural surroundings, and adjusted biological systems influence the conveyance of species and make new difficulties for protection. Resolving the interconnected issues of environmental change and untamed life exchange requires incorporated approaches that think about the more extensive ecological setting.

3. **One Wellbeing Approach:**

The One Wellbeing approach, perceiving the interconnectedness of human, creature, and ecological wellbeing, offers an extensive structure for tending to natural life wrongdoing. By grasping the connections between zoonotic infections, environment wellbeing, and unlawful natural life exchange, nations can foster comprehensive methodologies that advance both protection and general wellbeing.

6.1 Existing legal frameworks and international agreements

The fight against unlawful untamed life exchange requires a vigorous and facilitated legitimate system on both public and worldwide levels. Throughout the long term, huge endeavors have been made to make and fortify legitimate instruments that address the different aspects of this complicated issue. This article looks at the current lawful systems and peaceful accords that structure the foundation of the worldwide reaction to unlawful natural life exchange, investigating their advancement, viability, and difficulties.

1. **Show on Global Exchange Imperiled Types of Wild Fauna and Greenery (Refers to):**

1. **Establishment and Targets:**
The Show on Worldwide Exchange Imperiled Types of Wild Fauna and Verdure (Refers to) is a foundation of worldwide endeavors to control and screen global exchange jeopardized species. Laid out in 1973, Refers to expects to guarantee that global exchange doesn't undermine the endurance of wild creatures and plants. The show works on the guideline of reasonable use, perceiving the monetary worth of natural life while guaranteeing its preservation.

2. **Three Informative supplements:**
Refers to arranges species into three addendums in light of the degree of assurance they require. Addendum I incorporates species undermined with annihilation, and exchange these species is denied for principally business purposes. Addendum II incorporates species that might become imperiled on the off chance that their exchange isn't managed, requiring grants for worldwide exchange. Informative supplement III incorporates species subject to guideline in line with a party worried about their exchange.

3. **Viability and Difficulties:**

Refers to has been instrumental in checking the unlawful exchange of jeopardized species by giving a legitimate system to worldwide participation.

Nonetheless, challenges persevere, remembering variations for authorization limits among part nations, absence of subsidizing for powerful execution, and the developing idea of natural life wrongdoing. The show's viability relies upon the responsibility of part states to implement its arrangements.

II. Joined Countries Show Against Transnational Coordinated Wrongdoing (UNTOC) and its Conventions:

1. **The Palermo Show:**
The Unified Countries Show Against Transnational Coordinated Wrongdoing, otherwise called the Palermo Show, was taken on in 2000 to address different types of transnational coordinated wrongdoing. It perceives that untamed life wrongdoing frequently includes coordinated criminal organizations and incorporates conventions explicitly focusing on this issue. The show gives a complete system to battle the different features of transnational coordinated wrongdoing.

2. **Guns Convention:**
The Convention against the Unlawful Assembling of and Dealing with Guns, Their Parts and Parts and Ammo (Guns Convention) is one of the conventions

under the Palermo Show. While not straightforwardly centered around untamed life wrongdoing, this convention is important as the unlawful exchange guns is frequently connected to poaching and dealing exercises. By tending to the illegal weapons exchange, the convention by implication adds to battling untamed life wrongdoing.

3. **Viability and Difficulties:**

The Palermo Show and its conventions upgrade global participation and lawful devices for fighting coordinated wrongdoing, including untamed life dealing. Nonetheless, challenges emerge from the requirement for sanction by part states, shifting degrees of responsibility, and the advancing methodologies of criminal organizations. Fortifying the execution of these conventions requires proceeded with endeavors to construct limit and encourage cooperation.

III. The Show on Natural Variety (CBD):

1. **Targets and Standards:**
The Show on Natural Variety (CBD), embraced in 1992, expects to preserve organic variety, guarantee economical utilization of its parts, and advance the fair and impartial sharing of advantages emerging from hereditary assets. While not explicitly intended to address unlawful natural life exchange, the CBD perceives the significance of biodiversity protection and economical asset the board.

2. **Aichi Biodiversity Targets:**
The CBD laid out a bunch of objectives known as the Aichi Biodiversity Targets, which incorporate targets connected with the maintainable utilization of biodiversity, forestalling the eradication of compromised species, and fighting unlawful exchange. Target 12 explicitly addresses forestalling the termination of known compromised species and further developing their protection status, by implication adding to endeavors against untamed life wrongdoing.

3. **Adequacy and Difficulties:**

The CBD gives a structure to comprehensive biodiversity protection, recognizing the interconnectedness of biological systems and species. Be that as it may, challenges remember the requirement for additional particular arrangements for unlawful untamed life exchange, upgraded authorization instruments, and more prominent coordination of biodiversity protection into more extensive supportable advancement objectives.

IV. The World Traditions Association (WCO) and Refers to Coordinated effort:

1. **WCO-Refers to Natural life and Customs Drive:**
Perceiving the essential job of customs experts in fighting unlawful untamed

life exchange, the World Traditions Association (WCO) and Refers to laid out the WCO-Refers to Untamed life and Customs Drive. This coordinated effort means to upgrade the limit of customs authorities to identify and forestall unlawful exchange untamed life items. It gives preparing, rules, and instruments to reinforce customs requirement.

2. **Knowledge Sharing and Preparing Projects:**
The WCO-Refers to joint effort works with insight dividing between customs specialists universally. Preparing programs center around building the abilities of customs authorities in distinguishing, assessing, and holding onto unlawful natural life items. This drive upgrades the forefront protection against untamed life dealing by incorporating customs implementation into the more extensive legitimate system.

3. **Adequacy and Difficulties:**

The WCO-Refers to coordinated effort has been viable in building limit and advancing collaboration among customs specialists. Be that as it may, challenges incorporate the requirement for supported subsidizing, exhaustive preparation programs, and the mix of customs endeavors with more extensive policing.

V. Local Arrangements and Drives:

1. **ASEAN Natural life Requirement Organization (ASEAN-WEN):**
Provincial arrangements and drives assume a pivotal part in tending to unlawful untamed life exchange inside unambiguous geological regions. The ASEAN Natural life Requirement Organization (ASEAN-WEN) is an eminent model, uniting Southeast Asian countries to battle untamed life dealing. ASEAN-WEN works with insight sharing, joint tasks, and limit working among part nations.

2. **Territorial Joint effort in Africa:**
In Africa, territorial joint efforts, for example, the Lusaka Arrangement, mean to battle unlawful untamed life exchange. These arrangements work with composed endeavors among African nations to address the particular difficulties presented by natural life wrongdoing on the landmass. Provincial drives recognize the transboundary idea of unlawful exchange and underscore aggregate activity.

3. **Viability and Difficulties:**

Territorial arrangements and drives upgrade coordination among adjoining nations, considering more designated reactions to untamed life wrongdoing. Be that as it may, challenges remember abberations for assets and limits among part expresses, the requirement for orchestrated legitimate systems, and the advancing idea of criminal organizations working across locales.

VI. The Assembled Countries Office on Medications and Wrongdoing (UN-ODC) and its Worldwide Projects:

1. **UNODC and the Worldwide Program for Battling Natural life and Timberland Wrongdoing:**
   The Unified Countries Office on Medications and Wrongdoing (UNODC) assumes a focal part in tending to untamed life wrongdoing through its Worldwide Program for Fighting Untamed life and Woodland Wrongdoing. This drive centers around reinforcing legitimate systems, improving policing, and elevating global participation to battle unlawful natural life exchange.

2. **Support for Part States:**
   The UNODC offers help to part states as specialized help, limit building, and the improvement of thorough methodologies to address natural life wrongdoing. Its projects add to fortifying law enforcement frameworks, advancing law and order, and encouraging cooperation between policing.

3. **Viability and Difficulties:**

The UNODC's worldwide projects have been viable in building the limit of part states to battle natural life wrongdoing. Challenges incorporate the requirement for supported subsidizing, tending to the underlying drivers of unlawful exchange, and adjusting procedures to the developing strategies of criminal organizations.

VII. Public Regulation and Authorization:

1. **Fortifying Public Regulation:**
   Compelling public regulation is essential to fighting unlawful natural life exchange. Numerous nations have reinforced their regulations to line up with peaceful accords and give a powerful legitimate system to tending to natural life wrongdoing. Arrangements might incorporate severe punishments for wrongdoers, guidelines on exchange, and measures to safeguard imperiled species.

2. **Teams and Concentrated Units:**
   Nations frequently lay out committed teams and concentrated policing to address untamed life wrongdoing. These units center around knowledge get-together, examinations, and requirement activities connected with unlawful natural life exchange. Their development mirrors a guarantee to focusing on untamed life wrongdoing inside the more extensive range of policing.

3. **Viability and Difficulties:**

The adequacy of public regulation and authorization endeavors differs around the world. Challenges incorporate asset limitations, defilement inside policing, and the requirement for harmonization with worldwide lawful systems. Reinforcing homegrown limits and cultivating worldwide coordinated effort are fundamental parts of a complete methodology.

6.2 Successes and failures in combating rhino horn trafficking

The battle against rhino horn dealing is a complicated and progressing fight that includes a mix of worldwide collaboration, lawful systems, local area commitment, and mechanical developments. This paper looks at the victories and disappointments in fighting rhino horn dealing, featuring key accomplishments and diligent moves in the worldwide endeavors to safeguard these notorious and imperiled species.

1. **Achievements in Battling Rhino Horn Dealing:**
1. **Expanded Worldwide Mindfulness:**

   One remarkable progress as of late has been the uplifted global attention to the rhino horn exchange and its overwhelming effect on rhino populaces.

   Worldwide drives, mindfulness missions, and coordinated effort between legislatures, NGOs, and the confidential area have added to a more extensive comprehension of the dire need to safeguard rhinos from poaching and dealing.

2. **Fortified Legitimate Structures:**

   Numerous nations have found a way critical ways to fortify their lawful structures connected with natural life wrongdoing, remembering the unlawful exchange for rhino horns. Regulation with stricter punishments for poaching and dealing, as well as guidelines overseeing the exchange and transportation of rhino horn, has been carried out in a few locales. These legitimate measures plan to go about as obstructions and give a premise to indictment.

3. **Global Participation and Teams:**

   The foundation of worldwide teams and cooperative endeavors among nations have yielded positive outcomes. Associations like INTERPOL and the Assembled Countries Office on Medications and Wrongdoing (UNODC) have worked with data sharing, joint tasks, and limit building drives. These coordinated efforts upgrade the aggregate capacity to battle the coordinated lawbreaker networks associated with rhino horn dealing.

4. **Imaginative Innovation and Scientific Methods:**

   Headways in innovation, including the utilization of satellite following, DNA examination, and computerized stages, have demonstrated instrumental in the battle against rhino horn dealing. Untamed life legal sciences has turned into an amazing asset for policing, permitting them to follow the beginning of held onto horns, destroy dealing organizations, and construct more grounded bodies of evidence against culprits.

5. **Local area Commitment and Neighborhood Strengthening:**

Effective protection endeavors frequently include the dynamic support of neighborhood networks. Drives that enable networks living close to rhino natural surroundings, giving elective vocations, schooling, and motivations for safeguarding untamed life, have shown guarantee. At the point when networks become stewards of their regular assets, they assume an imperative part in forestalling poaching and dealing.

II. Disappointments and Tenacious Difficulties in Fighting Rhino Horn Dealing:

1. **Heightening Interest in Buyer Nations:**
   Regardless of endeavors to bring issues to light, interest for rhino horn perseveres in some customer nations, especially in pieces of Asia. Social convictions, customary medication rehearses, and the view of rhino horn as a superficial point of interest add to a rewarding underground market. Tending to the main drivers of interest stays a complicated test requiring supported schooling and mindfulness crusades.

2. **Debasement and Frail Administration:**
   Defilement inside nations embroiled in the rhino horn exchange stays a huge hindrance. From pay off of policing to complicit government specialists, defilement cultivates a climate where criminal organizations can work without risk of punishment. Reinforcing administration structures, advancing straightforwardness, and tending to defilement are pivotal parts of battling natural life wrongdoing really.

3. **Deficient Assets and Limit:**
   Numerous nations, particularly those with high rhino populaces, face asset imperatives and limit moves in their endeavors to battle dealing. Lacking subsidizing, obsolete hardware, and restricted faculty block the capacity of policing to watch immense and frequently far off rhino living spaces successfully. Fortifying assets and limit at both public and worldwide levels is fundamental.

4. **Advancing Strategies of Criminal Organizations:**
   Criminal organizations engaged with rhino horn dealing ceaselessly adjust their strategies to dodge policing. Complex carrying courses, the utilization of innovation to convey and arrange criminal operations, and the association of coordinated wrongdoing networks present continuous difficulties. Specialists should remain in front of these advancing strategies to disturb and destroy dealing networks successfully.

5. **Line Control and Transnational Nature:**

The transnational idea of rhino horn dealing makes successful line control basic. Notwithstanding, variations in line control limits among nations, permeable boundaries, and the utilization of numerous travel focuses by dealers confound endeavors to block and stop the unlawful exchange. Reinforcing worldwide collaboration in line control stays a squeezing challenge.

III. Proposals for Future Systems:

1. **Fortifying Global Coordinated effort:**
   The triumphs in fighting rhino horn dealing highlight the significance of supported worldwide coordinated effort. Nations should keep on sharing knowledge, coordinate joint tasks, and backing each other in legitimate structures and requirement endeavors. Reinforcing organizations with associations like INTERPOL, UNODC, and territorial teams is critical.

2. **Tending to Request through Training:**
   To handle the tenacious issue of interest, a proceeded with center around training and mindfulness crusades is fundamental. Focusing on purchaser nations with socially delicate informing, dissipating fantasies about the alleged restorative properties of rhino horn, and advancing elective materials for conventional practices can add to lessening interest.

3. **Enabling Neighborhood People group:**
   Putting resources into programs that engage neighborhood networks living close to rhino territories is critical to guaranteeing manageable preservation endeavors. Giving schooling, medical services, and elective vocations can cultivate a feeling of obligation and responsibility for, transforming networks into partners in the battle against poaching and dealing.

4. **Utilizing Innovation for Requirement:**
   Proceeded with interest in innovation, including progressed observation frameworks, drone innovation, and information examination, can altogether upgrade policing. Coordinating these devices into exhaustive systems considers more successful observing of rhino territories, early discovery of criminal operations, and further developed insight gathering.

5. **Fortifying Lawful Measures and Punishments:**

Nations need to consistently survey and reinforce their legitimate systems connected with rhino horn dealing. This incorporates returning to punishments for poaching and dealing, shutting lawful provisos, and guaranteeing that regulation stays up with advancing criminal strategies. Steady and powerful implementation of regulations is basic to going about as an obstruction

6.3 The need for collaborative efforts among nations

In an interconnected world confronting a bunch of perplexing difficulties, the requirement for cooperative endeavors among countries has never been more essential.

From ecological preservation and general wellbeing to monetary soundness and peacekeeping, worldwide issues rise above borders, requesting aggregate activity and shared liability. This exposition investigates the basic of cooperative endeavors among countries, stressing the effect of brought together drives in tending to worldwide difficulties.

1. **Natural Preservation and Environmental Change:**

1. **Transboundary Nature of Ecological Issues:**
   Ecological difficulties, for example, environmental change, deforestation, and biodiversity misfortune, perceive no international limits. The effects of natural corruption stretch out past individual countries, influencing biological systems, atmospheric conditions, and the prosperity of whole areas. Cooperative endeavors are fundamental for address the main drivers of natural issues and execute practical arrangements on a worldwide scale.
2. **Shared Assets and Obligations:**

Numerous natural difficulties include the common utilization of assets, like seas and the air. Countries should cooperate to reasonably oversee and save these assets. Peaceful accords, similar to the Paris Settlement on environmental change, epitomize the acknowledgment that an aggregate responsibility is expected to relieve the unfavorable impacts of natural corruption.

II. General Wellbeing and Worldwide Pandemics:

1. **Cross-Boundary Spread of Illnesses:**
   General wellbeing emergencies, like pandemics, highlight the interconnectedness of the worldwide local area. The fast spread of illnesses across borders features the requirement for cooperative endeavors in reconnaissance, data sharing, and composed reactions. Illnesses know no lines, making worldwide wellbeing security dependent upon the aggregate endeavors of countries.
2. **Immunization Appropriation and Access:**

The fair dispersion of antibodies during worldwide wellbeing emergencies requires coordinated effort among countries. Admittance to immunizations, therapies, and clinical assets ought to be comprehensive, perceiving that a solid world is one where each individual has the chance for wellbeing and prosperity. Cooperative drives, as COVAX, plan to guarantee fair admittance to antibodies around the world.

III. Financial Steadiness and Exchange:

1. **Relationship of Worldwide Economies:**
   The relationship of worldwide economies implies that monetary strength is dependent upon global collaboration. Economic deals, monetary guidelines, and cooperative financial strategies add to a stronger and adjusted worldwide monetary framework. Countries cooperating can address monetary difficulties, for example, downturns and monetary emergencies, all the more really.
2. **Destitution Mitigation and Practical Turn of events:**

Cooperative endeavors are critical for progressing practical advancement objectives and lightening neediness. Worldwide help, organizations, and information sharing add to engaging countries to lift their residents out of destitution. Perceiving the interconnectedness of improvement results cultivates a feeling of shared liability regarding the prosperity of all.

IV. Peacekeeping and Compromise:

1. **Aggregate Security and Strategy:**
   The support of worldwide harmony and security requires aggregate safety efforts and political endeavors. Global associations, for example, the Unified Countries, assume a focal part in interceding clashes, advancing discourse, and forestalling the heightening of strains into full-scale wars. Cooperative peacekeeping drives add to solidness and forestall the spread of viciousness.

2. **Compassionate Help and Outcast Emergencies:**

In the midst of contention and compassionate emergencies, cooperative endeavors are fundamental for giving ideal and successful philanthropic help. Countries cooperating can address displaced person streams, convey help, and backing the modifying of social orders impacted by struggle. The worldwide outcast emergency features the requirement for an organized reaction to guarantee the prosperity of dislodged populaces.

Chapter 7

Innovative Approaches

In the always developing scene of worldwide difficulties, imaginative methodologies are crucial for address complex issues that rise above borders. This article investigates different imaginative methodologies across assorted spaces, including innovation, medical care, training, and maintainability. By saddling imagination and utilizing state of the art arrangements, countries and associations can spearhead groundbreaking change and explore the complexities of the contemporary world.

1. **Development in Innovation:**
1. **Man-made brainpower and AI:**
   The mix of computerized reasoning (artificial intelligence) and AI (ML) has changed enterprises and critical thinking abilities. From medical care diagnostics to monetary estimating, computer based intelligence and ML calculations break down tremendous datasets, recognize designs, and create bits of knowledge that illuminate direction. These advancements can possibly improve proficiency, precision, and development across various areas.

2. **Blockchain Innovation:**
   Blockchain innovation, at first produced for digital currencies, has risen above its starting points to upset different fields. Its decentralized and straightforward nature guarantees secure, alter safe exchanges, making it priceless for areas, for example, finance, production network the board, and medical care. Blockchain cultivates trust, lessens misrepresentation, and presents additional opportunities for coordinated effort.

3. **Web of Things (IoT):**
   The Web of Things (IoT) associates gadgets, sensors, and frameworks to consistently trade data. In agribusiness, savvy cultivating utilizes IoT to improve crop the executives, while in metropolitan preparation, brilliant urban communities use IoT to upgrade framework and asset the board. The interconnectedness worked with by IoT drives effectiveness and manageability across enterprises.

4. 5G Innovation:

The coming of 5G innovation addresses a change in outlook in correspondence. Past giving quicker web speeds, 5G empowers the multiplication of shrewd gadgets, independent vehicles, and expanded reality encounters.

Its low dormancy and high data transmission open opportunities for inventive applications, changing how people, organizations, and states collaborate.

II. Medical care Advancement:

1. **Telemedicine and Distant Medical services:**
   Telemedicine has arisen as a groundbreaking arrangement, particularly with regards to worldwide wellbeing emergencies. Distant medical services administrations, empowered by computerized correspondence advancements, permit patients to talk with medical services experts, get conclusions, and access clinical guidance from the solace of their homes. This approach improves medical services availability and lessens the weight on actual foundation.

2. **Accuracy Medication:**
   Accuracy medication tailors clinical medicines to individual qualities, consolidating factors like hereditary qualities, way of life, and climate. Progresses in genomics and information examination empower medical care suppliers to offer customized therapy plans, working on the viability of treatments and limiting antagonistic impacts. Accuracy medication holds guarantee for more designated and proficient medical services intercessions.

3. **Wearable Innovation and Wellbeing Checking:**
   Wearable gadgets, going from smartwatches to wellness trackers, have become essential to individual wellbeing checking. These gadgets track indispensable signs, active work, and rest designs, engaging people to proactively deal with their wellbeing. The information gathered can likewise add to populace wellbeing studies, offering experiences into patterns and potential wellbeing gambles.

4. **Mechanical technology in Medical services:**

   Mechanical technology assumes a critical part in medical services, from surgeries to patient consideration. Careful robots empower accuracy and negligibly obtrusive methods, while assistive robots support people with handicaps. Computerization in medical care settings upgrades productivity and permits medical services experts to zero in on additional complicated errands, at last working on quiet results.

III. Advancements in Training:

1. **Web based Learning Stages:**
   Web based learning stages have democratized schooling, giving admittance to quality learning assets paying little mind to geological area.

Monstrous Open Internet based Courses (MOOCs), intelligent e-learning modules, and virtual study halls have changed conventional instructive ideal models. These developments upgrade openness, adaptability, and moderateness for students around the world.

2. **Gamification and Instructive Innovation:**

Gamification incorporates game components into instructive encounters to draw in students and improve inspiration. Instructive innovation stages influence gamified ways to deal with make learning more intelligent and pleasant. Computer generated reality (VR) and increased reality (AR) advances further enhance instructive encounters by establishing vivid learning conditions.

3. **Customized Learning:**

Customized learning tailors instructive substance to individual learning styles and needs. Versatile learning stages use information investigation to survey understudy execution, adjust example designs, and offer designated help. This approach encourages a more comprehensive instructive climate, obliging different learning inclinations and advancing understudy achievement.

4. **Cooperative Learning Instruments:**

Advanced instruments that work with cooperative learning have become indispensable to present day instruction. Virtual cooperation stages, online undertaking the board devices, and intelligent conversation gatherings empower understudies and teachers to participate in cooperative ventures, encouraging collaboration, decisive reasoning, and information sharing.

IV. Manageability and Ecological Development:

1. **Sustainable power Innovations:**

The change to sustainable power sources, for example, sun oriented and wind power, addresses an essential shift toward manageability. Developments in energy capacity, framework the board, and savvy advances upgrade the proficiency and dependability of sustainable power frameworks. These headways add to decreasing reliance on non-renewable energy sources and alleviating the effects of environmental change.

2. **Roundabout Economy Practices:**

The roundabout economy model intends to limit squander and advance asset productivity by reusing, reusing, and reusing materials. Developments in squander the board, feasible item plan, and eco-accommodating bundling add to making a more round and supportable monetary framework. This approach tends to ecological worries while supporting financial development.

3. **Reasonable Horticulture Advancements:**

Creative advances in farming advance reasonable works on, upgrading both efficiency and natural stewardship. Accuracy farming utilizes information examination, sensors, and IoT gadgets to enhance crop the board, lessen asset use, and limit ecological effect. Vertical cultivating and aqua-farming proposition effective options in contrast to customary agribusiness, saving area and water assets.

4. **Preservation Innovations:**

Mechanical developments are instrumental in preservation endeavors to safeguard biodiversity and biological systems. Robots and satellite imaging help in checking untamed life populaces and environment changes. Sensor networks give continuous information on ecological circumstances, assisting traditionalists with settling on informed choices. Protection advances add to safeguarding regular assets and advancing biological equilibrium.

V. Social Advancement and Local area Improvement:

1. **Social Business:**
   Social business consolidates business standards with a promise to tending to social and ecological difficulties. Developments in friendly undertakings center around making economical answers for cultural issues, going from neediness and training to medical services and natural preservation. Social business engages networks and cultivates comprehensive development.

2. **Local area drove Advancement:**
   Local area drove advancement underlines the dynamic contribution of nearby networks in molding and executing improvement drives. Participatory dynamic cycles, grassroots getting sorted out, and limit building enable networks to address their one of a kind difficulties. This approach guarantees that arrangements are logically applicable and feasible.

3. **Influence Financial planning:**
   Influence focusing on projects that create positive social and ecological results close by monetary returns. Financial backers look to have a significant effect on issues like destitution, training, and medical care while supporting imaginative plans of action. Influence effective money management adjusts monetary objectives to social and natural obligation.

4. **Open-Source Coordinated effort:**

Open-source coordinated effort includes the sharing of information, assets, and innovation for everyone's benefit. Activities, programming, and drives created through open-source coordinated effort permit assorted patrons overall to cooperate on normal difficulties. This comprehensive methodology cultivates development, speeds up critical thinking, and advances the democratization of data.

VI. Challenges and Moral Contemplations:

1. **Protection and Information Security:**

   The expansion of innovation and information driven arrangements raises worries about protection and information security. Advancements, for example, man-made intelligence and IoT include the assortment and examination of immense measures of individual information, requiring strong guidelines and moral systems to defend people's protection and forestall abuse of data.

2. **Imbalance and Access Differences:**

   While developments hold huge potential, there is a gamble of fueling existing disparities. Admittance to cutting edge innovations, quality medical care, and instruction might be unevenly conveyed, making computerized isolates and worsening differences. Moral contemplations should focus on inclusivity, guaranteeing that inventive arrangements benefit all sections of society.

3. **Natural Effect:**

   A few mechanical developments may incidentally add to ecological debasement through asset extraction, electronic waste, and energy utilization. A comprehensive way to deal with development ought to consider life-cycle evaluations, economical plan standards, and the natural effect of arising innovations to limit environmental impressions.

4. **Moral Utilization of artificial intelligence and Robotization:**

The arrangement of simulated intelligence and computerization in different enterprises raises moral worries connected with work removal, predisposition in calculations, and the capable utilization of independent frameworks. Moral contemplations should direct the turn of events and execution of these advancements to guarantee that their advantages are circulated evenhandedly and that they line up with cultural qualities.

7.1 Technology and its role in conservation and anti-poaching efforts

The constant dangers to worldwide biodiversity, exacerbated by poaching and territory obliteration, require imaginative ways to deal with protection. In this specific situation, innovation arises as a strong partner in the battle against natural life violations and the safeguarding of jeopardized species. This paper investigates the complex job of innovation in preservation and hostile to poaching endeavors, looking at how headways in different fields add to the security of natural life and environments.

1. **Reconnaissance and Observing Advances:**

1. **Drones:**

   Automated airborne vehicles, generally known as robots, have altered untamed life checking and against poaching endeavors. Furnished with high-goal cameras and warm imaging, drones give continuous observation of immense and distant regions. Preservationists use robots to screen creature populaces, track poachers, and evaluate living space conditions, empowering more compelling and convenient mediations.

2. **Satellite Innovation:**

Satellite innovation assumes a urgent part in checking and overseeing untamed life territories for a huge scope. Remote detecting satellites give important information on deforestation, natural surroundings misfortune, and changes in land cover. Preservation associations influence this data to recognize regions under danger, plan protection systems, and track the developments of jeopardized species.

3. **Camera Traps:**

Camera traps, furnished with movement sensors, catch pictures or recordings of untamed life in their normal environments. These gadgets offer non-meddling observing, permitting specialists to concentrate on creature conduct, gauge populace estimates, and recognize individual creatures. Camera traps have become fundamental devices in grasping slippery species and identifying criminal operations in safeguarded regions.

II. Information Examination and Man-made consciousness:

1. **Prescient Examination:**

Information examination, energized by progressions in man-made consciousness (computer based intelligence), empowers traditionalists to foresee and forestall untamed life wrongdoings. By dissecting verifiable information on poaching episodes, environment infringement, and human-natural life clashes, prescient investigation can recognize high-risk regions and guide the distribution of assets for designated mediations.

2. **AI for Picture Acknowledgment:**

AI calculations are progressively utilized for picture acknowledgment in preservation endeavors. These calculations can examine tremendous datasets of pictures caught by camera traps or robots, naturally distinguishing and arranging untamed life species. This smoothes out the examination interaction as well as adds to more precise populace evaluations.

3. **Acoustic Observing:**

Consolidating AI, acoustic observing frameworks examine sounds in common habitats to recognize and distinguish natural life vocalizations. This innovation permits scientists to screen the presence of explicit species, track movement examples, and even distinguish trouble calls, helping with hostile to poaching endeavors and preservation arranging.

III. Against Poaching Innovations:

1. **GPS Following:**
   Worldwide Situating Framework (GPS) GPS beacons are appended to creatures to screen their developments continuously. Moderates use GPS following to concentrate on movement designs, comprehend living space use, and identify surprising way of behaving that might show misery or poaching. This innovation upgrades the capacity to answer quickly to likely dangers.

2. **Brilliant Fencing and Sensors:**
   Shrewd fencing frameworks, furnished with sensors and alerts, give an extra layer of insurance for untamed life. These frameworks can distinguish gatecrashers, including poachers, and ready experts continuously. Savvy walls are especially viable in high-risk regions where customary fencing might be deficient.

3. **Untamed life DNA Investigation:**

Headways in DNA examination add to fighting untamed life dealing. By gathering and investigating DNA tests from seized items, for example, ivory or rhino horns, specialists can follow the beginning of the poached creatures. DNA data sets work with the ID of poaching areas of interest and the destroying of unlawful untamed life exchange organizations.

IV. Local area Commitment and Correspondence Advancements:

1. **Portable Applications for Revealing:**
   Portable applications engage neighborhood networks and untamed life aficionados to partake in preservation endeavors effectively. Announcing applications permit clients to submit data about untamed life sightings, dubious exercises, or potential poaching occurrences. This publicly supported information improves the proficiency of hostile to poaching watches and cultivates a feeling of shared liability.

2. **Correspondence Organizations:**
   Laying out dependable correspondence networks in remote and weak regions is essential for planning against poaching endeavors. Satellite correspondence, radio organizations, and versatile availability empower officers, policing, protection associations to share ongoing data, answer occurrences, and direction crisis mediations.

3. **Training and Mindfulness Stages:**

Innovation works with the dispersal of instructive materials and mindfulness missions to advance preservation values. Sites, online entertainment stages, and computer generated reality encounters draw in crowds around the world, encouraging comprehension of the significance of untamed life preservation and the outcomes of criminal operations.

V. Challenges and Moral Contemplations:

1. **Security Concerns:**
   The broad utilization of reconnaissance advances raises worries about individual protection, especially in regions where nearby networks coincide with untamed life. Finding some kind of harmony between protection endeavors and regarding the privileges and security of native populaces is significant to building trust and accumulating nearby help.

2. **Information Security:**
   The assortment and investigation of huge measures of information, remembering touchy data for untamed life and environments, require vigorous information safety efforts. Protecting against unapproved access and digital dangers is fundamental to forestall the abuse of important preservation information.

3. **Openness and Moderateness:**
   While state of the art advances hold massive potential, their far reaching reception might be prevented by issues of availability and reasonableness. Guaranteeing that protection advancements are open to different networks and associations, particularly those in asset compelled locales, stays a test.

4. **Moral Utilization of simulated intelligence:**

The sending of man-made reasoning in preservation raises moral contemplations, especially in examples where artificial intelligence is utilized to settle on choices with expected lawful or ecological results. Guaranteeing straightforwardness, decency, and responsibility in computer based intelligence applications is imperative to moral protection rehearses.

VI. Future Patterns and Coordination:

1. **Coordination of Advancements:**
   The fate of protection lies in the combination of different advancements to make extensive and synergistic arrangements. Consolidating satellite information with on-the-ground sensors, coordinating artificial intelligence with customary following strategies, and utilizing the qualities of various advances will improve the general adequacy of preservation endeavors.

2. **Tech Development Centers for Preservation:**
   Laying out advancement centers that unite technologists, protectionists, and nearby networks can drive the improvement of setting explicit innovations. These center points can act as stages for cooperative examination, trial and error, and the co-production of arrangements that address explicit protection challenges.

3. **Resident Science and Innovation:**
   The ascent of resident science drives, empowered by innovation, permits people to add to preservation endeavors effectively. From examining camera trap pictures to taking part in untamed life observing applications, innovation engages

residents to become basic supporters of logical exploration and preservation projects.

4. **Arising Innovations:**

Progressions in quantum registering, mechanical technology, and bioengineering hold guarantee for tending to preservation challenges in clever ways. Quantum registering can deal with complex environmental models all the more productively, mechanical technology can upgrade hands on work and checking capacities, and bioengineering might offer creative answers for species recuperation.

7.2 Community-based conservation initiatives

Local area based protection drives address a change in outlook in the way to deal with safeguarding biodiversity and environments. By perceiving the essential job nearby networks play in the maintainable administration of regular assets, these drives engage individuals to become stewards of their surroundings. This paper dives into the standards, methodologies, and effect of local area based protection, featuring how cultivating cooperation among networks and preservation endeavors prompts more viable and economical results.

1. **Standards of Local area Based Preservation:**
1. **Local area Commitment and Interest:**
   At the center of local area based preservation is dynamic local area commitment and support. As opposed to forcing hierarchical preservation gauges, these drives include neighborhood networks in dynamic cycles, drawing on their customary information and guaranteeing that their requirements and yearnings are thought of.
2. **Strengthening and Limit Building:**
   Local area put together protection centers with respect to engaging neighborhood networks to take responsibility for endeavors. This includes limit working through schooling, preparing, and the exchange of abilities. Engaged people group are better prepared to go with informed choices, carry out reasonable practices, and effectively add to preservation objectives.
3. **Social Awareness and Regard:**
   Perceiving and regarding the social variety of networks is basic to the outcome of these drives. By recognizing native information and social practices, local area based preservation embraces a comprehensive methodology that coordinates conventional insight with contemporary protection techniques.
4. **Shared Advantages and Motivating forces:**

Local area based protection stresses the evenhanded sharing of advantages got from preservation exercises. This incorporates monetary motivators, for example, income sharing systems or maintainable job potential open doors, which rouse networks to partake in and support preservation drives effectively.

II. Systems for Local area Based Preservation:

1. **Co-The executives of Regular Assets:**
   Co-the board includes joint effort between nearby networks, government offices, and preservation associations in the maintainable use and assurance of normal assets.
   This approach perceives the significance of adjusting preservation objectives with the financial requirements of networks, cultivating a feeling of shared liability.

2. **Local area Oversaw Safeguarded Regions:**
   Engaging people group to deal with their own safeguarded regions is a critical system in local area based preservation. This includes giving neighborhood networks the power and obligation to administer and safeguard assigned regions, guaranteeing that protection endeavors line up with the necessities and goals of individuals living inside or close to these areas.

3. **Supportable Job Drives:**
   Coordinating practical business drives into protection programs helps address the financial necessities of nearby networks. This might incorporate eco-accommodating the travel industry, crafted works, or supportable farming undertakings that turn out elective revenue sources while advancing natural maintainability.

4. **Instruction and Mindfulness:**

Instruction is an integral asset for building mindfulness and cultivating a preservation ethic inside networks. Local area based protection drives put resources into instructive projects that feature the significance of biodiversity, environmental cycles, and the job networks can play in defending their regular legacy.

III. Examples of overcoming adversity and Effect of Local area Based Preservation:

1. **Contextual investigation: Namibian People group Conservancies**
   Namibia's People group Conservancy Program remains as a fruitful illustration of local area based preservation. This drive engages country networks to oversee and profit from untamed life and normal assets. Conservancies have the position to oversee natural life, the travel industry, and different exercises inside their areas, prompting expanded biodiversity, further developed occupations, and a feeling of satisfaction and possession among local area individuals.

2. **Contextual analysis: Agroforestry in Guatemala**
   In Guatemala, people group based agroforestry drives have added to both

protection and financial maintainability. Native people group are effectively associated with reforestation endeavors, integrating different tree species into rural scenes. This approach upgrades biodiversity, further develops soil wellbeing, and furnishes networks with practical wellsprings of lumber, natural products, and non-wood timberland items.

3. **Influence on Biodiversity Preservation:**
   Local area based preservation drives decidedly affect biodiversity protection. At the point when networks are effectively taken part in preservation endeavors, they go about as overseers of neighborhood environments, adding to the security of imperiled species, rebuilding of living spaces, and by and large natural wellbeing.

4. **Social and Monetary Advantages:**

The financial advantages of local area based preservation are complex. By giving networks financial impetuses, for example, income from practical the travel industry or fair-exchange certificate for items, these drives add to destitution lightening, further developed occupations, and the production of manageable monetary other options.

IV. Difficulties and Contemplations:

1. **Outside Tensions and Land Use Change:**
   Networks participated in protection frequently face outside pressures, including infringement for farming or foundation advancement. Adjusting protection objectives with the financial necessities of developing populaces requires cautious preparation and cooperation to forestall land use changes that might sabotage preservation endeavors.

2. **Restricted Assets and Limit:**
   Numerous people group come up short on assets and limit expected to execute preservation drives successfully. Restricted admittance to training, innovation, and monetary assets can frustrate the progress of local area based programs, accentuating the significance of outer help and limit building measures.

3. **Clashes and Administration Issues:**
   At times, clashes might emerge inside networks or among networks and outside partners over asset the board and preservation rehearses. Viable administration structures, compromise systems, and clear correspondence are vital for address these difficulties and guarantee the manageability of local area based preservation drives.

4. **Evolving Financial Elements:**

Worldwide and nearby financial elements, for example, market requests and environmental change, can influence the outcome of local area based protection drives. Adaptability and versatile administration techniques are significant to address developing difficulties and guarantee the proceeded with importance and viability of protection endeavors.

V. Future Headings and Proposals:

1. **Reinforcing Associations:**
   Building solid associations between nearby networks, government offices, non-administrative associations (NGOs), and the confidential area is fundamental for the outcome of local area based protection. Cooperative endeavors tackle different skill, assets, and viewpoints, encouraging an all encompassing and coordinated way to deal with preservation.

2. **Supporting Native Information:**
   Perceiving and supporting native information frameworks is indispensable for the outcome of local area based protection drives. Native people group frequently have important experiences into reasonable asset the board rehearses and natural strength, adding to the general adequacy of preservation endeavors.

3. **Putting resources into Instruction and Limit Building:**
   Putting resources into schooling and limit working inside networks is a drawn out procedure for manageable preservation. By giving admittance to preparing, innovation, and information, networks can foster the abilities expected to take part in and lead preservation drives effectively.

4. **Tending to Environmental Change Effects:**

Environmental change presents critical difficulties to protection endeavors, influencing biological systems and the livelihoods of neighborhood networks. Local area based protection drives ought to consolidate environment versatile procedures, for example, manageable land-use practices and variation measures, to address the effects of an evolving environment.

7.3 Creative strategies to reduce demand for rhino horns

The determined interest for rhino horns represents a grave danger to these glorious animals, driving unlawful poaching and adding to the downfall of rhino populaces around the world. Tending to this challenge requires rigid policing protection endeavors as well as innovative systems to handle the underlying driver: request. This paper investigates inventive methodologies and innovative techniques pointed toward diminishing the interest for rhino horns, consequently adding to the safeguarding of these notorious species.

1. **Public Mindfulness Missions:**
   Saddling the force of training and mindfulness, public missions assume a vital part in modifying discernments and ways of behaving. Imaginative and effective informing through different stations, including web-based entertainment, TV, and local area occasions, can scatter legends encompassing the restorative

properties of rhino horns and accentuate the staggering results of poaching on rhino populaces. Connecting with visuals, narrating, and tributes can summon sympathy, encouraging a feeling of obligation among general society.

2. **Instructive Projects in Customary Medication:**
Teaming up with specialists of conventional medication to teach them about the real essence of rhino horns can be instrumental in checking request. Studios, courses, and instructive materials that give precise data about other option, feasible fixings in customary medication can assist with moving discernments inside these networks. By advancing moral and harmless to the ecosystem rehearses, this approach tends to request at its source.

3. **Big name Supports and Powerhouse Missions:**
Utilizing the impact of big names and virtual entertainment powerhouses can intensify hostile to rhino poaching messages. Connecting notable figures out in the open help declarations, supports, or virtual entertainment crusades contacts an expansive crowd as well as adds validity to the reason. The profound association that VIPs can lay out with their supporters can encourage a more grounded obligation to protection values.

4. **Maintainable Business Drives:**
Making elective types of revenue for networks implied in or in danger of taking part in unlawful untamed life exchange can assist with diminishing the financial motivators driving rhino horn interest. Maintainable business drives, for example, eco-accommodating the travel industry, handiwork creation, or local area based preservation projects, give networks practical other options, tending to the underlying drivers of their association in poaching exercises.

5. **Strategic Commitment and Global Cooperation:**
Taking part in conciliatory endeavors to address the interest for rhino horns on a global scale is urgent. Teaming up with nations where request is high to implement stricter guidelines and punishments for unlawful untamed life exchange can be successful. Furthermore, cultivating worldwide associations for knowledge sharing and joint policing upgrades the worldwide obligation to fighting the unlawful rhino horn exchange.

6. **Corporate Social Obligation (CSR) Drives:**
Empowering organizations to take a position against the unlawful untamed life exchange and backing protection endeavors through CSR drives can be effective. Organizations, particularly those with binds to areas where rhino horn request is high, can put resources into protection projects, support hostile to poaching drives, or bring issues to light inside their client base. Such drives add to preservation as well as upgrade an organization's standing for social obligation.

7. **Blockchain Innovation for Detectability:**

Utilizing blockchain innovation can bring straightforwardness and detectability into the store network, making it more challenging for unlawful items to enter the market. By making an evident and unchanging record of the rhino horn exchange, this innovation can stop purchasers, as they become more mindful of the moral ramifications related with the unlawful untamed life exchange.

Chapter 8

Stories From The Frontline

The fight against rhino poaching is pursued day to day on the bleeding edges of protection, where committed people stand up to the cruel real factors of unlawful untamed life exchange. This assortment of stories dives into the existences of those at the front of the battle - preservationists, officers, and nearby networks - revealing insight into their difficulties, wins, and the resolute obligation to safeguarding rhinos and their territories.

1. **The Protectionist's Point of view:**
1. **The Call of Nature:**
   Meet Sarah Thompson, an enthusiastic preservationist whose affection for untamed life drove her to devote her life to rhino protection. From her initial days concentrating on nature to the difficult hands on work in Africa, Sarah's process is one of flexibility and responsibility. She shares the delights of seeing rhino conduct right at home and the profound cost of experiencing the consequence of poaching episodes.
2. **Developments in Protection:**
   Investigate the tale of Dr. Raj Patel, a preservation researcher pushing the limits of development. Driven by a longing to use innovation for protection, he created state of the art arrangements, for example, man-made intelligence fueled enemy of poaching robots and acoustic observing frameworks. His account mirrors the convergence of energy, science, and innovation in the continuous battle to safeguard rhinos.
3. **Cooperative Preservation:**

Join Emma Mbatha, a local area commitment subject matter expert, as she underscores the significance of cooperation among progressives and neighborhood networks. Emma's methodology includes building trust, grasping neighborhood viewpoints, and consolidating local area driven arrangements. Her encounters feature the extraordinary effect of cooperative preservation on both untamed life and human prosperity.

II. The Officer's Fearlessness:

1. **Life on the Bleeding edge:**
Step into the boots of Jackson Sibanda, an officer positioned in a rhino hold. Jackson gives a firsthand record of the difficulties and risks looked by officers in their everyday work. From following poachers in the thick shrub to shielding rhinos from hurt, his story enlightens the mental fortitude and penance expected to protect these lofty animals.

2. **Kinship in the Wild:**
Investigate the very close local area of officers through the eyes of Maria Nkosi, a carefully prepared officer with an abundance of involvement. Maria's story digs into the brotherhood among officers, the common obligation regarding safeguarding natural life, and the profound cost of seeing the effect of poaching. Her story mirrors the versatility and fortitude that supports officers on the cutting edge.

3. **The Concealed Legends:**

Meet Joseph Mwamba, a reconnaissance master whose abilities in following and observing are vital to hostile to poaching endeavors. Joseph's story features the frequently ignored job of reconnaissance in safeguarding rhinos. From deciphering creature conduct to recognizing likely dangers, his skill contributes altogether to the progress of hostile to poaching tasks.

III. Networks as Watchmen:

1. **Watchmen of the Land:**
Find the tale of the Nkosi family, whose genealogical land is home to a rhino populace. As caretakers of the land, the Nkosi family relates their excursion of coinciding with natural life, adjusting the requirements of their local area with the basic to safeguard rhinos. Their story highlights the fundamental job nearby networks play in preservation.

2. **Enabling the Future:**
Follow the story of Samuel Chansa, a teacher locally lining a public park. Samuel's endeavors center around instructing the more youthful age about the significance of protection. Through school projects and local area drives, he expects to impart a feeling of obligation and pride in protecting rhinos and their living spaces among the young.

3. **Maintainable Vocations:**

Investigate the tale of Kabelo Molefe, a local area pioneer carrying out economical work drives. Kabelo's methodology includes making monetary choices that decrease dependence on poaching. From eco-accommodating the travel industry to moral cultivating rehearses, his endeavors exhibit how engaging networks financially adds to rhino protection.

IV. Stories of Win and Difficulties:

1. **Fruitful Intercessions:**
   Find out about the victories of Dr. Jane Muthoni, a veterinarian driving fruitful mediations in rhino protection. Dr. Muthoni's encounters range from fruitful rhino movements to the recovery of harmed rhinos. Her account features the basic job of veterinary aptitude in guaranteeing the prosperity of rhino populaces.

2. **Conquering Misfortune:**
   Experience the tale of Peter Ngwenya, an officer who confronted misfortune in the line of obligation. Peter's record subtleties the difficulties of recuperating from an experience with poachers and the mental cost of seeing the effect of poaching on rhinos. His strength and assurance epitomize the individual penances made by those on the forefronts.

3. **Progressing Difficulties:**

Explore the continuous difficulties looked by Laura Mbeki, a protection advocate attempting to address official holes and implement stricter punishments for poaching. Laura's account reveals insight into the intricacies of exploring lawful systems, tending to debasement, and pushing for strategy changes to reinforce the battle against rhino poaching.

8.1 Personal narratives of individuals impacted by rhino horn trafficking

Rhino horn dealing, driven by interest for indicated restorative and superficial point of interest purposes, has expansive outcomes that reach out past the untamed life preservation domain. This assortment of individual accounts plans to reveal insight into the human element of this emergency, investigating the narratives of people whose lives have been personally moved by the staggering impacts of rhino horn dealing. Through these stories, we try to convey the earnestness of tending to the interest for rhino horns and its significant effect on individuals, networks, and the more extensive social texture.

1. **The Poacher's Situation:**
1. **From Neediness to Poaching:**
   Meet Samuel Mbeki, a previous poacher who went to unlawful untamed life exchange out of franticness. Samuel's story follows his excursion from destitution to poaching, featuring the monetary constrains that drive people to take part

in criminal operations. His story highlights the mind boggling interaction of financial variables that add to the propagation of rhino horn dealing.

2. **The Close to home Cost:**
   Investigate the inner strife experienced by Maria Khumalo, a poacher's better half. Maria's story dives into the mental and profound cost of living with a spouse participated in criminal operations. She describes the steady feeling of dread toward captures, the ethical problem looked by her family, and the inescapable feeling of weakness that goes with a day to day existence entwined with natural life wrongdoing.

3. **Restoration and Reclamation:**

Follow the narrative of David Nkosi, a restored poacher turned protection advocate. David's story reveals insight into the conceivable outcomes of restoration and recovery for people caught in the pattern of poaching. His process mirrors the extraordinary force of training, local area commitment, and elective work amazing open doors in breaking the chains of rhino horn dealing.

II. Families Destroyed:

1. **Misfortune and Sadness:**
   Enter the universe of the Simelane family, who encountered the disastrous loss of a friend or family member because of contribution in rhino horn dealing. Their story subtleties the close to home consequence, the sorrow that wrapped the family, and the dependable effect on connections. Through their story, we witness the significant human expense of unlawful untamed life exchange.

2. **Criticism and Disconnection:**
   Find out about the difficulties looked by Jessica Dlamini, the sister of an individual sentenced for rhino horn dealing. Jessica's account investigates the social shame and segregation experienced by families associated with natural life wrongdoing. Her story highlights the requirement for local area backing and understanding to break the pattern of detachment and work with reintegration.

3. **Youngsters Abandoned:**

Investigate the tale of Ntombi Mthembu, a single parent whose spouse was captured for rhino horn dealing. Ntombi's story digs into the battles of bringing kids alone up in the fallout of a relative's contribution in criminal operations. Her story features the more extensive cultural ramifications and weaknesses looked by youngsters in such conditions.

III. Untamed life Dealing and Native People group:

1. **Removal and Social Disintegration:**
   Meet Boss Themba Zulu, a head of a native local area dislodged because of the

infringement of natural life dealing. Boss Zulu's account unfurls the difficulties looked by native networks compelled to leave their tribal terrains. The relocation disturbs customary lifestyles as well as adds to the disintegration of social legacy.

2. **Loss of Jobs:**
   Investigate the effect of natural life dealing on the jobs of the Xhosa people group through the eyes of Nomvula Mabaso. Nomvula's story explains the financial outcomes of rhino horn dealing, which upsets customary jobs like horticulture and specialties.
   The story mirrors the more extensive monetary weaknesses looked by native networks at the front of this emergency.

3. **Local area Drove Protection:**

Find the story of Bongani Ndlovu, a local area pioneer supporting protection drives. Bongani's story exhibits the potential for local area drove protection endeavors to address the double difficulties of natural life dealing and the conservation of native lifestyles. Through cooperative undertakings, networks can assume a crucial part in safeguarding untamed life while supporting their social legacy.

IV. The Authorities: Policing Lawful Results

1. **Officer's Penance:**
   Step into the boots of Daniel Khumalo, a devoted officer focused on safeguarding rhinos. Daniel's account investigates the penances made by people on the forefront of implementation, itemizing the physical and close to home cost of going up against poachers. His story mirrors the enduring commitment of those putting their lives in extreme danger to protect untamed life.

2. **Lawful Repercussions:**
   Investigate the lawful repercussions looked by Sipho Mbele, an untamed life dealer sentenced for rhino horn pirating. Sipho's story digs into the intricacies of legitimate outcomes, revealing insight into the analytical cycle, court procedures, and the more extensive effect of lawful intercessions on natural life wrongdoing. His story gives bits of knowledge into the difficulties of upholding regulations against natural life dealing.

3. **Debasement and Complicity:**

Dive into the story of Analyst Thabo Moloi, who examines the complicity of authorities in rhino horn dealing. Thabo's story uncovers the difficulties of battling defilement inside policing and accentuates the significance of addressing interior debasement to reinforce hostile to dealing endeavors.

V. Promoters and Activists: Voices for Change

1. **Survivor Turned Promoter:**
   Follow the excursion of Lindiwe Mhlongo, an overcomer of rhino horn dealing who presently advocates against the exchange. Lindiwe's account describes her frightening experience, the most common way of recuperating, and her assurance to bring issues to light about the results of natural life dealing. Her story embodies the flexibility of survivors turned advocates.
2. **Local area Assembly:**
   Investigate the local area assembly endeavors drove by extremist Thando Sibeko. Thando's account features the force of grassroots developments in bringing issues to light, impacting strategy, and assembling networks against rhino horn dealing. Her story embodies the effect of aggregate activity in driving positive change.
3. **Global Cooperation:**

Find out about the endeavors of Dr. Jamal Malik, a worldwide backer teaming up to battle rhino horn dealing. Dr. Malik's story highlights the significance of worldwide collaboration, associations among countries, and the job of global associations in tending to the interest for rhino horns. His story represents the interconnected idea of natural life dealing and the need of a bound together reaction.

VI. Trust for What's to come: Preservation Examples of overcoming adversity

1. **Rhino Recovery:**
   Find the recovery excursion of Thandi, a rhino who endure a poaching assault. Thandi's story, told through the eyes of her guardians, mirrors the expectation and versatility that rise out of fruitful recovery endeavors. Her story represents the potential for positive change and the effect of protection drives on individual lives.
2. **Local area Drove Protection Drives:**
   Investigate the outcome of local area drove preservation drives in the Amakhala Game Hold. Through the accounts of local area individuals, officers, and traditionalists, witness the extraordinary force of cooperative endeavors in safeguarding rhinos and cultivating supportable conjunction among natural life and networks.
3. **Schooling and Mindfulness:**

Find out about the effect of schooling and mindfulness programs drove by Dr. Effortlessness Ndlovu. Dr. Ndlovu's account underlines the job of training in evolving discernments, cultivating sympathy, and tending to the interest for rhino horns. Her story represents the potential for long haul change through educated and caring networks.

8.2 Accounts from law enforcement, conservationists, and local communities

The battle against rhino horn dealing includes a different cluster of people, each assuming a one of a kind part in tending to this worldwide emergency. This thorough assortment of firsthand records gives an inside and out investigation of the points of view of policing, protectionists, and nearby networks. Through their accounts, we gain knowledge into the difficulties, wins, and cooperative endeavors that characterize the continuous battle to safeguard rhinos from the illegal exchange of their horns.

1. **Policing:**
1. **On the Cutting edges:**
   Join Official John Makoni as he relates his encounters on the bleeding edges of the fight against rhino poaching. From following poachers through provoking landscapes to participating in high-stakes secret tasks, Official Makoni's story gives a firsthand glance at the risks and intricacies looked by policing focused on safeguarding rhinos.
2. **The Job of Insight:**
   Investigate the record of Criminal investigator Sandra Ndlovu, a knowledge official having some expertise in untamed life wrongdoing. Analyst Ndlovu's story dives into the basic job of knowledge gathering in distinguishing and destroying coordinated rhino horn dealing organizations. Her story uncovers the perplexing snare of criminal activities and the essential measures utilized by policing.
3. **Joint effort Across Boundaries:**

Step into the shoes of Assessor Rafael Hernandez, an official engaged with global coordinated effort to battle rhino horn dealing. Auditor Hernandez's story unfurls the difficulties and accomplishments of cross-line participation, stressing the need of shared knowledge, facilitated endeavors, and global associations in tending to the transnational idea of natural life wrongdoing.

II. Preservationist Viewpoints:

1. **The Biological Effect:**
   Meet Dr. Sarah Williams, a preservation researcher committed to understanding the natural outcomes of rhino poaching. Dr. Williams' account investigates the flowing impacts on biological systems, from upset pecking orders to changed vegetation elements, accentuating the interconnectedness of rhino populaces with more extensive natural wellbeing.
2. **Preservation Innovation:**
   Dive into the universe of Dr. Raj Singh, a preservation technologist spearheading the utilization of state of the art innovation in rhino security. Dr. Singh's account reveals the job of robots, camera traps, and different developments in observing rhino populaces, recognizing poaching exercises, and giving significant information to protection techniques.

3. **Challenges in Recovery:**

Follow the encounters of Dr. Emily Harris, a veterinarian work in the restoration of rhinos impacted by poaching occurrences. Dr. Harris' account reveals insight into the physical and inner difficulties of restoring rhinos, from getting wounds tending to mental injury, and the intricacies of once again introducing them into their regular territories.

III. Voices from Neighborhood People group:

1. **Native Viewpoints:**
   Enter the universe of Boss Ndlovu, a pioneer from a native local area living in closeness to rhino territories. Boss Ndlovu's account verbalizes the fragile harmony between protection endeavors and the financial requirements of native networks, underlining the significance of consolidating native information and points of view in preservation systems.

2. **Maintainable Occupations:**
   Investigate the drives drove by Amina Jalloh, a local area coordinator upholding for reasonable vocations as an option in contrast to rhino poaching. Amina's story uncovers the extraordinary effect of engaging networks financially, giving suitable options that add to both protection objectives and further developed occupations.

3. **Instruction and Mindfulness:**

Join Instructor Mbeki on her excursion to teach nearby networks about the significance of rhino preservation. Educator Mbeki's story highlights the job of schooling and mindfulness in cultivating a feeling of obligation and pride inside networks, making an establishment for reasonable conjunction among people and rhinos.

IV. Converging Accounts: Cooperative Endeavors

1. **The Force of Joint effort:**
   Investigate the cooperative endeavors of Reviewer Zhang Wei from China, working pair with global partners to address the interest for rhino horns. Examiner Zhang's story mirrors the interconnected idea of the rhino horn exchange, underscoring the significance of joint endeavors to battle both organic market.

2. **Local area Drove Preservation:**
   Find the examples of overcoming adversity rising up out of local area drove protection drives, where policing, and neighborhood networks meet. Through accounts from local area individuals, officers, and preservationists, witness the groundbreaking force of cooperative undertakings in safeguarding rhinos and cultivating manageable concurrence.

3. **Difficulties and Wins:**

Explore the record of Dr. Maria Duarte, a progressive confronting the difficulties of offsetting biological safeguarding with the necessities of nearby networks. Dr. Duarte's story uncovers the intricacies and wins of settling on some mutual interest, showing the continuous endeavors to make an amicable connection between protection drives and local area prosperity.

V. The Human Cost: Individual Accounts

1. **Survivor Stories:**
   Investigate the tales of survivors like Nkosi, a previous poacher who got some distance from an existence of wrongdoing. Nkosi's story mirrors the potential for restoration and reclamation, outlining the human cost of association in rhino horn dealing and the opportunities for positive change.

2. **Families Affected:**
   Meet Beauty Mwamba, a mother wrestling with the results of her child's contribution in the unlawful natural life exchange. Beauty's story dives into the profound and social repercussions experienced by families impacted by rhino horn dealing, stressing the requirement for help instruments and local area understanding.

3. **From Poaching to Assurance:**

Follow the excursion of Thabo Nkosi, a transformed poacher currently working close by policing safeguard rhinos. Thabo's story features the intricacies of individual change, revealing insight into the moves and inspirations that drive people to move from poaching to preservation backing.

VI. Progressing Difficulties and Future Viewpoints:

1. **Regulative Holes:**
   Investigate the difficulties looked by Backer Fatima Malik, a legitimate master attempting to address official holes in untamed life wrongdoing implementation. Advocate Malik's story highlights the significance of legitimate systems and the requirement for thorough and severe regulations to battle rhino horn dealing actually.

2. **Environmental Change Effect:**
   Find the points of view of Dr. Luis Mendez, an environment researcher looking at the effect of environmental change on rhino territories. Dr. Mendez's account stresses the interconnected dangers looked by rhinos, joining the difficulties of environmental change with the continuous tensions of poaching and dealing.

3. **Arising Arrangements:**

Uncover the inventive arrangements proposed by Dr. Mei Ling, a scientist reading up arising innovations for rhino insurance. Dr. Mei Ling's story investigates the capability of hereditary advancements, observation frameworks, and global cooperation as future-situated procedures to counter rhino horn dealing.

8.3 Inspirational stories of successful conservation and anti-trafficking initiatives

Even with the worldwide test presented by rhino horn dealing, various people and associations have adapted to the situation, exhibiting versatility, development, and steadfast responsibility. This gathering of moving stories dives into effective preservation and hostile to dealing drives that have had a significant effect in the fight to safeguard rhinos. These stories grandstand the victories, methodologies, and cooperative endeavors that have prepared for positive change, giving expectation and motivation to a future where rhinos flourish in their regular natural surroundings.

1. **Activity Rainstorm: An Organized Global Exertion**

   In the core of the unlawful untamed life exchange, Activity Tempest remains as a demonstration of the force of global joint effort. Led by INTERPOL and including policing from 92 nations, this drive designated the whole unlawful production network, from source nations in Africa to travel and objective nations in Asia. The activity brought about more than 1,800 captures and the capture of incalculable rhino horns, ivory, and other unlawful untamed life items. The outcome of Activity Rainstorm highlights the significance of worldwide collaboration in handling the mind boggling, transnational nature of untamed life dealing.

2. **RhODIS: DNA Innovation for Rhino Assurance**

   Headways in DNA innovation have turned into an impressive device in the battle against rhino poaching. The Rhinoceros DNA List Framework (RhODIS) is an imaginative drive that uses DNA profiling to make an extensive data set of individual rhinos. Created by the College of Pretoria's Veterinary Hereditary qualities Lab, RhODIS plays had a critical impact in connecting recuperated rhino horns to explicit crime locations, helping with the ID and indictment of poachers and dealers. This mechanical advancement embodies the convergence of science and preservation in defending rhinos.

3. **Namibian People group Protection: A Model for Concurrence**

   Namibia stands apart as a reference point of outcome in local area drove preservation endeavors. Through drives like the Collective Conservancy Program, neighborhood networks are engaged to oversee and profit from untamed life assets, including rhino populaces.

   The program gives monetary motivators through dependable eco-the travel industry and natural life based undertakings, encouraging a feeling of pride and shared liability regarding rhino preservation. Namibia's people group driven approach fills in as a model for supportable conjunction among individuals and untamed life.

4. **Old Pejeta Conservancy: Advancements in Untamed life Security**
In Kenya, the Good old Pejeta Conservancy has arisen as a spearheading force in untamed life protection. The conservancy utilizes state of the art innovations, like robot observation, to screen rhino populaces and recognize possible dangers. Furthermore, the mix of local area commitment programs guarantees the help of neighborhood occupants in the preservation endeavors. Old Pejeta's all encompassing methodology, consolidating innovation, local area inclusion, and hearty safety efforts, embodies an exhaustive procedure to safeguard rhinos.

5. **Kaziranga Public Park: A Safe-haven for Indian Rhinos**
Kaziranga Public Park in India has been a wonderful example of overcoming adversity in the protection of the Indian one-horned rhinoceros. Thorough enemy of poaching measures, including the utilization of prepared elephants and furnished watches, have added to a critical decrease in rhino poaching occurrences. Besides, people group based protection drives and effective movement programs have extended rhino natural surroundings, guaranteeing a solid future for the populace. Kaziranga's accomplishments highlight the significance of a complex methodology in safeguarding jeopardized rhino species.

6. **The Dark Mambas: All-Female Enemy of Poaching Unit**
In South Africa, the Dark Mambas stand as an image of strengthening and flexibility even with rhino poaching. Including ladies from nearby networks, this all-female enemy of poaching unit watches the Balule Nature Hold, effectively captivating with networks to bring issues to light about preservation. The Dark Mambas' non-fierce methodology underlines instruction and local area outreach, testing conventional thoughts of hostile to poaching endeavors. Their story grandstands the extraordinary capability of comprehensive, local area driven protection drives.

7. **Rhino Protection Lab in Vietnam: Forming Perspectives**
Tending to the interest for rhino horns includes changing social perspectives and dissipating legends encompassing their restorative properties. The Rhino Protection Lab in Vietnam has been at the very front of this work, using schooling, effort, and mindfulness missions to reshape public discernments.
By drawing in with conventional medication specialists, the lab pursues advancing moral other options and underlining the protection basic. The lab's drives feature the significance of tending to request side elements in the battle against rhino horn dealing.

8. **WildAid's Missions: Affecting Buyer Conduct**
WildAid, a worldwide protection association, has been instrumental in utilizing public attention to drive change in buyer conduct. Through high-profile crusades highlighting famous people, WildAid has contacted crowds in key interest markets, including China and Vietnam. These missions expect to decrease the interest for rhino horns by scattering fantasies, bringing issues to light about the

outcomes of untamed life dealing, and advancing the requirement for preservation. WildAid's creative methodology highlights the force of promotion in molding cultural perspectives toward rhino horn utilization.

9. **Key Legitimate Mediations: Prevention and Indictment**
In the lawful domain, vital mediations play had a critical impact in deflecting and indicting people engaged with rhino horn dealing. High-profile cases and rigid lawful measures, like expanded punishments and fortified requirement, send a strong message about the seriousness of untamed life wrongdoings. Legitimate specialists and backers pursuing shutting provisos, further developing regulation, and guaranteeing the compelling execution of hostile to dealing regulations contribute essentially to the fight in court against rhino horn dealing.

10. **The Worldwide Walk for Elephants, Rhinos, and Lions: Promotion in real life**

The Worldwide Walk for Elephants, Rhinos, and Lions is a grassroots development that prepares individuals overall to advocate for the insurance of imperiled untamed life. Through walks, petitions, and mindfulness occasions, the development calls for more grounded lawful measures, global collaboration, and uplifted endeavors to battle untamed life dealing. The aggregate voice of activists and concerned residents enhances the call for horrific act, putting tension on states and partners to focus on the protection of rhinos.

Chapter 9

Looking Ahead

As we stand at the intersection of natural preservation, the test presented by rhino horn dealing requests premonition, development, and supported responsibility. This extensive investigation dives into the future points of view and systems that hold guarantee in the continuous fight to shield rhinos from the risks of unlawful untamed life exchange. From state of the art advances to strategy headways, local area strengthening to worldwide joint efforts, this examination means to give a guide to a future where rhinos can flourish as one with their biological systems.

1. **Mechanical Advancements: Molding the Eventual fate of Rhino Insurance**
1. **Man-made brainpower in Enemy of Poaching Endeavors:**
   The coordination of man-made reasoning (man-made intelligence) and AI advances holds monstrous potential in changing enemy of poaching endeavors. Savvy reconnaissance frameworks controlled by man-made intelligence calculations can dissect immense measures of information, identifying designs characteristic of potential poaching exercises. Drones furnished with cutting edge sensors and computer based intelligence capacities can give constant checking of rhino environments, empowering fast reaction to dangers. These mechanical headways introduce another period of proactive, information driven preservation.
2. **Hereditary Advancements for Rhinoceros Distinguishing proof:**
   Headways in hereditary advances, for example, high level DNA profiling and criminological examination, offer strong apparatuses for rhinoceros ID. By extending and refining information bases like the Rhinoceros DNA File Framework (RhODIS), protectionists can improve their capacity to follow the starting points of held onto rhino horns and connection them to explicit crime locations. This hereditary methodology helps with policing as well as adds to the general comprehension of rhino populaces and their hereditary variety.
3. **Blockchain Innovation for Straightforward Stock Chains:**

Blockchain innovation, known for its straightforwardness and unchanging nature, can be utilized to make a detectable and responsible inventory network for untamed life items. Applying blockchain to the rhino horn exchange could make it more challenging for unlawful items to enter the market, as each exchange would be recorded and apparent to pertinent specialists. This decentralized methodology can possibly upset the unlawful inventory network and lessen the interest for rhino horns.

II. Local area Strengthening: An Economical Methodology

1. **Local area Drove Protection Drives:**
   Engaging nearby networks to become stewards of their regular assets stays a foundation of reasonable preservation. Drives that include networks in natural life the executives, give financial other options, and focus on schooling add to an agreeable conjunction among individuals and rhinos. Contextual analyses from effective local area drove protection programs highlight the significance of this methodology in getting the drawn out prosperity of the two networks and natural life.

2. **Moral The travel industry as a Preservation Instrument:**
   The travel industry can be a strong power for preservation when drawn nearer morally and economically. Laying out and advancing natural life amicable the travel industry drives produces pay for neighborhood networks as well as brings issues to light about the significance of safeguarding rhinos and their environments. Vital associations between protection associations, neighborhood organizations, and the travel industry administrators can make encounters that benefit the two guests and the environments they investigate.

3. **Schooling and Promotion in Neighborhood People group:**

Putting resources into training and support inside nearby networks is urgent for moving social perspectives and diminishing the interest for rhino horns. Outreach programs that draw in schools, local area pioneers, and conventional healers can disperse legends encompassing the alleged restorative properties of rhino horns. By cultivating a feeling of satisfaction in nearby biodiversity and underlining the environmental significance of rhinos, these drives add to a grassroots development for protection.

III. Strategy and Lawful Intercessions: Reinforcing the Legitimate System

1. **Stricter Punishments for Natural life Dealing:**
   Improving legitimate structures to force stricter punishments for untamed life dealing sends a reasonable message about the gravity of these violations. Policymakers can attempt to reexamine and refresh existing regulation to guarantee that those engaged with rhino horn dealing face serious results. Global

collaboration in blending lawful principles and removal arrangements reinforces the obstruction impact of legitimate measures.

2. **Shutting Authoritative Holes:**
   Tending to authoritative holes that accidentally work with natural life dealing is significant for powerful authorization. Policymakers can team up with legitimate specialists, protection associations, and policing to recognize and redress shortcomings in current regulations.

   This incorporates guaranteeing that punishments are proportionate with the scale and effect of natural life violations, and that lawful structures give adequate position to arraigning people associated with rhino horn dealing.

3. **Connecting with Native and Nearby Information in Arrangement Development:**

Integrating native and nearby information frameworks into strategy arrangement is fundamental for making socially pertinent and viable protection methodologies. Perceiving the customary jobs of networks in natural life the executives and coordinating their experiences into policymaking processes encourages a feeling of pride and shared liability. Policymakers can work cooperatively with native pioneers to foster arrangements that line up with both protection objectives and local area values.

IV. Worldwide Coordinated effort: Reinforcing Worldwide Organizations

1. **Insight Sharing and Joint Activities:**
   Improving knowledge dividing and coordination among nations is principal in tending to the transnational idea of rhino horn dealing. Cooperative endeavors, for example, joint activities and teams, work with the trading of data between policing. Interpol, territorial associations, and two-sided arrangements assume a vital part in reinforcing worldwide organizations, making a unified front against natural life wrongdoing.

2. **Conciliatory Measures and Endorses:**
   Strategic channels can be utilized to address the interest for rhino horns in key shopper markets. Nations with critical interest can be urged to execute and implement stricter guidelines against the exchange, and discretionary strain can be applied to guarantee consistence. The burden of authorizations on countries that neglect to resolve the issue can act as a strong motivator for global participation.

3. **Support for Agricultural Nations:**

Agricultural nations frequently endure the worst part of the difficulties presented by rhino horn dealing, remembering asset imperatives and the effect for neighborhood networks. Worldwide cooperation ought to incorporate monetary and specialized help for these countries, empowering them to execute viable preservation measures, reinforce policing, and put resources into local area based drives.

V. Moving Social Stories: Changing Perspectives and Request

1. **Public Mindfulness Missions:**

   Extensive public mindfulness crusades are instrumental in testing social stories that drive the interest for rhino horns. By utilizing assorted media stages, these missions can scatter exact data about the biological significance of rhinos, the lawlessness of the exchange, and the moral options in contrast to customary medication.

   Joint efforts with powerhouses, VIPs, and social symbols enhance the compass and effect of these drives.

2. **Drawing in Conventional Medication Experts:**

   Cooperative endeavors with customary medication specialists can assume a crucial part in moving social mentalities. Exchanges and organizations with healers and specialists can prompt a superior comprehension of elective cures and the expulsion of rhino horns from customary solutions. Training and mindfulness programs custom fitted to these networks add to a more educated and dependable way to deal with conventional medication.

3. **Financial Choices for Craftsmans:**

   Giving financial options in contrast to craftsmans participated in creating items from rhino horns is fundamental for decreasing the interest for such things. Drives that help the advancement of feasible livelihoods, elective materials, and market access for craftsmans add to breaking the pattern of reliance on untamed life items. Financial strengthening lines up with the standards of protection and local area prosperity.

VI. Preservation Notwithstanding Environmental Change: Versatile Methodologies

1. **Environment Tough Protection Arranging:**

   Environmental change represents extra difficulties to untamed life protection, influencing living spaces, water sources, and vegetation. Preservation techniques should be versatile and environment tough, taking into account the possible changes in biological systems and the effect on rhino populaces. Cooperative exploration and observing endeavors can illuminate protection arranging that expects and addresses the natural outcomes of environmental change.

2. **Cross-Species Protection Techniques:**

   The interconnectedness of biological systems requires comprehensive protection moves toward that think about the necessities of different species. Coordinating rhino protection endeavors with more extensive biodiversity protection drives guarantees the conservation of whole environments. Cross-species preservation methodologies cultivate natural equilibrium, alleviating the flowing impacts of rhino horn dealing on other greenery.

3. **Exploration and Checking for Versatile Administration:**

Interest in continuous examination and observing is vital for versatile administration methodologies. Traditionalists can utilize information on rhino conduct, populace elements, and natural surroundings changes to illuminate continuous navigation.

Mechanical developments, for example, satellite following and sensor organizations, add to a more profound comprehension of rhino biology and empower versatile administration because of arising dangers.

9.1 Future prospects for rhino populations

The fate of rhino populaces is at a basic point, formed by the interchange of natural, cultural, and protection elements. This investigation digs into the possibilities for rhino populaces, inspecting the difficulties they face and the procedures that deal expect their supported presence. From environment protection to imaginative preservation draws near, this examination means to illustrate the way ahead for these notorious and imperiled species.

1. **Protection Examples of overcoming adversity: A Brief look at Trust**
1. **Rhino Safe-havens and Stores:**
    The foundation and compelling administration of rhino asylums and holds have demonstrated to be instrumental in getting the fate of rhino populaces. Models like the Lewa Untamed life Conservancy in Kenya and Hluhluwe-iMfolozi Park in South Africa grandstand the progress of committed protection spaces. These stores give safeguarded living spaces to rhinos as well as act as habitats for research, local area commitment, and supportable the travel industry, adding to their drawn out practicality.
2. **Movement and Renewed introduction Projects:**
    Movement and renewed introduction programs have been vital in extending rhino populaces and reintegrating them into their verifiable reaches. Drives like the Dark Rhino Reach Extension Venture in South Africa and the Indian Rhino Vision 2020 in Assam, India, feature the progress of painstakingly arranged movement endeavors. These projects mean to lay out new populaces, improve hereditary variety, and relieve the dangers related with segregated populaces.
3. **Local area Drove Preservation Drives:**

Engaging neighborhood networks to effectively take part in rhino preservation has arisen as an extraordinary methodology. Drives like the Namibian Shared Conservancy Program and the Dark Mambas Hostile to Poaching Unit in South Africa epitomize the positive effect of local area drove preservation. By incorporating nearby information, giving monetary motivators, and encouraging a feeling of pride, these projects make a feasible structure for conjunction among networks and rhinos.

II. Challenges Not too far off: Dangers to Rhino Populaces

1. **Poaching and Unlawful Natural life Exchange:**
   Poaching stays the most prompt and serious danger to rhino populaces. Regardless of worldwide endeavors to control unlawful natural life exchange, interest for rhino horns continues in a few Asian business sectors, driven by conventional convictions and status imagery. The complexity of poaching organizations, filled by coordinated wrongdoing, represents a consistent test to requirement organizations and requires progressing endeavors to destroy these organizations.

2. **Territory Misfortune and Discontinuity:**
   Territory misfortune and discontinuity keep on reducing the accessible space for rhino populaces. As human populaces grow and scenes are changed, rhinos face difficulties in getting to reasonable natural surroundings for taking care of, reproducing, and relocation. The results of territory discontinuity incorporate expanded human-natural life struggle, decreased hereditary variety, and compromised environmental versatility.

3. **Environmental Change Effects:**

Environmental change represents a danger to rhino populaces by modifying their natural surroundings and influencing the accessibility of water and food assets. Changes in temperature, precipitation examples, and vegetation elements can upset environments, making it significant to consolidate environment versatile preservation methodologies. The requirement for versatile administration becomes basic to address the developing difficulties presented by an evolving environment.

III. Imaginative Preservation Systems: Preparing Forward

1. **High level Observing Innovations:**
   The mix of cutting edge observing advancements, like satellite following, robots, and sensor organizations, gives continuous information on rhino conduct, populace elements, and expected dangers. These advancements empower traditionalists to screen huge regions proficiently, identify poaching episodes speedily, and gain experiences into rhino developments and environmental communications.

2. **Genomic Protection and Helped Proliferation:**
   Propels in genomic advancements offer new roads for traditionalists to oversee and protect hereditary variety inside rhino populaces. Procedures like in vitro preparation (IVF) and planned impregnation add to the hereditary strength of populaces by working with rearing in controlled conditions. Genomic

preservation endeavors expect to make hereditary vaults, guaranteeing the accessibility of different hereditary material for future rearing projects.

3. **Local area Based The travel industry and Reasonable Vocations:**

The improvement of local area based the travel industry drives gives a reasonable type of revenue for neighborhood networks while at the same time cultivating preservation endeavors. Projects like the Sera Rhino Safe-haven Local area Conservancy in Kenya exhibit the capability of the travel industry as a device for monetary strengthening and preservation schooling. By connecting local area jobs to the prosperity of rhino populaces, these drives make a commonly valuable relationship.

IV. Strategy and Promotion: Fortifying Protection Structures

1. **Global Joint effort and Arrangements:**
   Reinforcing worldwide cooperation through arrangements and shows is pivotal for tending to the worldwide idea of rhino protection. Instruments like the Show on Global Exchange Jeopardized Types of Wild Fauna and Verdure (Refers to) assume a crucial part in directing the exchange of rhino horns and other natural life items. Deliberate endeavors among countries, upheld by powerful peaceful accords, are fundamental to make a brought together front against poaching and dealing.

2. **Stricter Legitimate Measures and Obstructions:**
   The requirement of stricter legitimate measures and impediments is foremost to deter people engaged with rhino horn dealing. Policymakers can upgrade punishments for natural life violations, further develop requirement capacities, and guarantee the compelling execution of against dealing regulations. Legitimate systems need to develop to address arising difficulties and give a strong groundwork to indicting those participated in criminal operations.

3. **Public Mindfulness and Promotion Missions:**

Public mindfulness missions and promotion endeavors assume a critical part in gathering support for rhino preservation. Associations like Save the Rhino and the Global Rhino Establishment take part in broad mindfulness missions to teach general society about the dangers confronting rhinos and the significance of protection. By preparing popular assessment and creating support, these missions add to expanded financing, strategy consideration, and aggregate activity.

V. Cooperative Exploration: Propelling Preservation Science

1. **Research on Rhino Conduct and Biology:**
   Proceeded with research on the way of behaving and biology of rhinos is key to figuring out their necessities, ways of behaving, and associations inside their biological systems. Bits of knowledge acquired from such examination illuminate

preservation methodologies, environment the board, and hostile to poaching endeavors.

Cooperative examination drives including researchers, environmentalists, and nearby networks add to a comprehensive comprehension of rhino populaces.

2. **Arising Advances in Preservation:**
   The investigation of arising advances, for example, blockchain for straightforward inventory chains and computer based intelligence for prescient demonstrating, offers imaginative answers for preservation challenges. Blockchain innovation can make straightforward and discernible stock chains, while artificial intelligence can investigate immense datasets to foresee potential poaching areas of interest. Incorporating these advances into preservation rehearses upgrades productivity and increases the viability of against poaching drives.

3. **Conduct Studies for Human-Natural life Concurrence:**

Understanding human-natural life conjunction is fundamental for alleviating clashes and advancing agreeable cooperations among networks and rhinos. Conduct concentrates on that inspect both human and rhino ways of behaving contribute important bits of knowledge to foster systems that lessen the gamble of contention. By encouraging conjunction, these examinations offer a plan for maintainable preservation rehearses that benefit both untamed life and networks.

VI. Global Financing and Backing: Putting resources into Preservation

1. **Monetary Help for Protection Drives:**
   Global subsidizing assumes a urgent part in supporting protection drives, particularly in emerging nations with rhino populaces. Givers, charitable associations, and global offices can offer monetary help for against poaching endeavors, natural surroundings rebuilding, local area strengthening, and exploration programs. Interest in protection exhibits an aggregate obligation to saving rhino populaces and their environments.

2. **Limit Building and Preparing Projects:**
   Building the limit of nearby networks, preservation associations, and policing is fundamental for the powerful execution of protection techniques. Preparing programs that improve abilities in enemy of poaching, natural surroundings the board, and local area commitment engage people and associations to assume a proactive part in rhino protection.

3. **Preservation The travel industry and Gathering pledges:**

Protection the travel industry, when overseen capably, can act as a huge wellspring of financing for rhino preservation. Drives like eco-the travel industry and natural life safaris draw in guests, producing income that can be reinvested in protection endeavors.

Raising money crusades, upheld by charitable organizations and corporate sponsorships, further add to the monetary supportability of progressing protection drives.

9.2 The role of education and awareness in curbing demand

In the fight against rhino horn dealing, tending to the interest side of the situation is all around as urgent as carrying out severe enemy of poaching measures. Training and mindfulness drives assume a crucial part in reshaping social mentalities, dispersing legends, and encouraging a feeling of obligation among buyers. This investigation dives into the multi-layered parts of instruction and mindfulness crusades, looking at their effect on controling interest for rhino horns and adding to the more extensive objectives of preservation.

1. **Grasping the Underlying foundations of Interest:**
1. **Social Insights and Customs:**
   Interest for rhino horns is well established in social discernments and customs, especially in specific Asian nations where they are accepted to have therapeutic properties. Understanding the verifiable and social settings that have molded these convictions is fundamental. By digging into the foundations of interest, training drives can tailor their ways to deal with successfully challenge and change these well established discernments.
2. **Status Imagery and Notoriety:**

Past customary convictions, rhino horns are additionally pursued as superficial points of interest and distinction things. The unique case and saw selectiveness of rhino horns add to their allure among specific socioeconomics. Training endeavors need to address the fundamental inspirations driving the interest, including the mental and social factors that drive people to look for these items.

II. The Force of Information: Dispersing Legends and Confusions

1. **Therapeutic Properties and Rhino Horns:**
   One of the essential drivers of interest for rhino horns is the confidence in their restorative properties. Instructive missions should efficiently expose these legends, introducing logical proof that verifies the absence of restorative viability in rhino horns. Teaming up with clinical experts, researchers, and moderates, these drives can give precise data that challenges the instilled misguided judgments encompassing the implied recuperating properties of rhino horns.
2. **Elective Medication and Protection:**

Instructive endeavors ought to underscore the accessibility of moral and economical options in customary medication. Featuring the extravagance of elective cures that don't include the utilization of jeopardized species adds to a change in shopper conduct. By advancing the utilization of natural, plant-based, or manufactured other options, instruction crusades cultivate a more mindful way to deal with customary medication that lines up with preservation targets.

III. Focusing on Key Socioeconomics: Fitting Directives for Effect

1. **Metropolitan Shoppers and Prosperous Business sectors:**
   In metropolitan communities and rich business sectors where interest for rhino horns is in many cases concentrated, designated instructive missions can have a huge effect. These drives ought to address the distinction among customers and the ecological outcomes of their decisions. Using a blend of media stages, including online entertainment, TV, and print, takes into consideration a broad dispersal of data that challenges the cultural standards related with rhino horn utilization.

2. **Youth Commitment and Future Promoters:**

Drawing in the adolescent is basic for long haul change. Instructive projects in schools, colleges, and public venues can impart a feeling of natural stewardship and sympathy for untamed life. Youth commitment drives might incorporate instructive studios, preservation centered educational programs, and extracurricular exercises that urge understudies to become advocates for natural life security. Engaging the cutting edge is critical to breaking the pattern of interest.

IV. Cooperative Organizations: Saddling the Force of Collusions

1. **Joint effort with Preservation Associations:**
   Schooling and mindfulness crusades benefit enormously from coordinated effort with laid out preservation associations. These associations intensify the scope of drives, taking advantage of existing organizations, and utilizing the ability of associations devoted to natural life assurance. Joint endeavors can incorporate the improvement of instructive materials, public help declarations, and local area outreach programs.

2. **Association of Big names and Forces to be reckoned with:**

The association of big names and forces to be reckoned with can altogether improve the perceivability and effect of schooling efforts. Utilizing the compass and impact of notable characters helps catch public consideration and scatter messages generally. VIP supports, public help declarations, and online entertainment crusades drove by forces to be reckoned with add to changing cultural discernments and mentalities toward rhino horn utilization.

V. The Job of Innovation: Creative Ways to deal with Schooling

1. **Computer generated Reality (VR) and Increased Reality (AR):**
   Creative advancements like computer generated simulation (VR) and expanded

reality (AR) offer vivid instructive encounters. VR can ship clients to rhino territories, giving a firsthand perspective on the creatures right at home. AR applications can overlay data about rhinos and the outcomes of poaching onto certifiable situations. These innovations make a strong vehicle for schooling that reverberates with present day crowds.

2. **Online Stages and Virtual Entertainment:**

The universality of online stages and virtual entertainment presents an unmatched chance for instruction missions to contact worldwide crowds. Connecting with content, including recordings, infographics, and intuitive elements, can be spread through stages like YouTube, Instagram, and Facebook. Web-based entertainment forces to be reckoned with and preservation supporters can use their web-based presence to bring issues to light and advance dependable purchaser conduct.

VI. Local area Contribution: Engaging Nearby Voices

1. **Local area Based Studios and Occasions:**
   Neighborhood people group in regions impacted by rhino horn dealing can assume critical part in training endeavors. Local area based studios and occasions work with direct communication, permitting instructors to fit messages to neighborhood social settings. These drives enable networks to take responsibility for objectives and become advocates for rhino assurance inside their locales.

2. **Coordinated effort with Customary Healers:**

Drawing in with conventional healers is fundamental, given their impact in networks where the utilization of rhino horns in customary medication is pervasive. Cooperative drives can include discoursed, studios, and instructional meetings that encourage a comprehension of elective cures and feasible practices. By building organizations with conventional healers, instruction crusades add to a social shift away from rhino horn use.

VII. Estimating Effect: Assessing the Adequacy of Schooling Drives

1. **Reviews and Social Investigations:**
   To evaluate the viability of training efforts, overviews and social examinations can be directed to quantify changes in information, perspectives, and ways of behaving. Pre-and post-crusade overviews give significant bits of knowledge into the effect of instructive endeavors on designated socioeconomics. Conduct studies can dissect shifts in shopper decisions and social practices after some time.

2. **Coordinated effort with Exploration Foundations:**

Working together with research foundations empowers the assessment of training drives utilizing thorough logical strategies. Analysts can configuration studies to gauge the mental, profound, and conduct results of instruction crusades. These associations add to prove based approaches, refining systems in view of true information and guaranteeing consistent improvement.

VIII. Difficulties and Contemplations: Exploring Intricacies

1. **Aversion to Social Variety:**
   Schooling efforts should move toward the variety of social convictions with responsiveness. Recognizing and regarding social subtleties is significant for building trust and guaranteeing that messages resound with assorted crowds. Fitting instructive substance to explicit social settings forestalls the inconvenience of outside points of view and encourages a cooperative way to deal with preservation.

2. **Long haul Responsibility and Subsidizing:**

Maintained and steady endeavors are expected for schooling efforts to impact enduring change. Long haul responsibility from legislatures, NGOs, and generous associations guarantees the coherence of instructive drives. Getting subsidizing for progressing efforts, exploration, and local area commitment is crucial for keeping up with energy and accomplishing supported influence.

IX. Examples of overcoming adversity: Observing Positive Change

1. **Decrease Sought after in Unambiguous Business sectors:**
   Examples of overcoming adversity from designated markets where interest for rhino horns has diminished exhibit the adequacy of training efforts. Dissecting situations where purchaser ways of behaving have moved, prompting a decrease popular, gives important experiences into the elements that add to fruitful results. These examples of overcoming adversity act as encouraging signs and motivation for progressing endeavors.

2. **Expanded Public Help for Protection:**

Schooling and mindfulness drives can add to a more extensive social change for protection. Expanded public help for preservation strategies, stricter guidelines, and moral buyer decisions demonstrate a developing familiarity with the interconnectedness between human exercises and natural prosperity. The arrangement of public feeling with preservation objectives reinforces the establishment for supported assurance of rhino populaces.

X. Looking Forward: A Dream for Mindful Commercialization

1. **Economical Practices and Moral Commercialization:**
   A definitive objective of schooling and mindfulness crusades is to encourage a culture of dependable and moral industrialism. Empowering people to settle on decisions that line up with protection standards, support manageable practices, and reject items got from natural life dealing adds to a future where rhinos can flourish without the danger of interest driven double-dealing.
2. **Worldwide Coordinated effort for Enduring Effect:**

Looking forward, the worldwide local area should strengthen cooperative endeavors to address the interest for rhino horns thoroughly. By saddling the force of training, innovation, local area inclusion, and worldwide organizations, a unified front can be shaped against the social and financial powers that drive rhino horn dealing. The vision for what's in store includes an existence where training has changed perspectives, making a practical conjunction among people and rhinos.

9.3 Recommendations for policymakers, NGOs, and the public

The preservation of rhinos is an intricate test that requires purposeful endeavors from policymakers, non-legislative associations (NGOs), and the general population. To resolve the multi-layered issues encompassing rhino horn dealing, embracing a thorough and cooperative approach is fundamental. This conversation frames key suggestions for every partner gathering to contribute really to the preservation and insurance of rhino populaces.

1. **Policymakers:**
1. **Reinforce Official Measures:**
   Policymakers assume a crucial part in forming the lawful system overseeing natural life preservation and dealing. To check rhino horn dealing, it is basic to fortify and uphold authoritative measures. This incorporates forcing stricter punishments for poaching and untamed life dealing, shutting legitimate provisos, and guaranteeing that regulations are similar with the gravity of these wrongdoings. Policymakers ought to consistently reconsider and refresh guidelines to stay up with advancing difficulties.
2. **Upgrade Global Collaboration:**
   Rhino horn dealing is a transnational issue that requires worldwide coordinated effort. Policymakers ought to effectively take part in strategic endeavors to encourage collaboration between nations impacted by the exchange. This includes reinforcing existing arrangements, working with data sharing, and empowering joint activities to destroy criminal organizations associated with the unlawful natural life exchange.
3. **Put resources into Hostile to Poaching and Authorization:**

Designating assets to hostile to poaching endeavors and policing is basic for combatting rhino horn dealing. Policymakers ought to focus on financing for preparing, gear, and innovation to improve the capacities of those on the bleeding edge. By putting resources into the strengthening of officers and policing, policymakers can make a more imposing protection against poaching exercises.

II. Non-Administrative Associations (NGOs):

1. **Support People group Drove Preservation Drives:**
   NGOs assume a critical part in supporting and carrying out local area drove protection drives. By engaging nearby networks to effectively take part in rhino protection, NGOs can cultivate a feeling of pride and obligation. This might include putting resources into training programs, giving elective occupations, and teaming up with networks to foster feasible practices that benefit the two individuals and untamed life.

2. **Store Exploration and Observing:**
   Exploration and observing are major parts of successful protection methodologies. NGOs can contribute by financing logical exploration on rhino conduct, territory elements, and the effects of poaching. Furthermore, supporting observing advancements, for example, satellite following and sensor organizations, empowers continuous information assortment, upgrading the comprehension of rhino populaces and working with versatile administration.

3. **Raise Public Mindfulness:**

NGOs assume a vital part in raising public mindfulness about the outcomes of rhino horn dealing. Through effective missions, instructive drives, and joint efforts with powerhouses, NGOs can spread precise data, disperse fantasies, and support mindful buyer decisions. Public help collected through mindfulness missions can, thusly, impact policymakers and add to a social change in perspectives toward rhino protection.

III. The general population:

1. **Settle on Informed Purchaser Decisions:**
   People have the ability to impact interest through their purchaser decisions. General society ought to effectively look for data about the moral and natural ramifications of items, including conventional medications. Settling on informed decisions and dismissing items got from rhino horn or other natural life upholds moral commercialization and adds to diminishing interest.

2. **Take part in Protection Drives:**
   Commitment to preservation drives, whether through chipping in, supporting neighborhood associations, or taking part in local area based projects, permits the general population to contribute straightforwardly to rhino security. By

effectively partaking in protection endeavors, people become advocates for change and enhance the effect of more extensive drives.

3. **Support Feasible The travel industry:**

The travel industry, when overseen capably, can be a strong power for protection. The general population can uphold maintainable the travel industry rehearses that focus on untamed life insurance and advance moral collaborations with rhinos. Picking eco-accommodating visit administrators and upholding for dependable the travel industry rehearses add to the monetary prosperity of neighborhood networks and the protection of rhino natural surroundings.